Mapping Autonomy in Language Education

FOREIGN LANGUAGE TEACHING IN EUROPE

Edited by
Manuel Jiménez Raya, Terry Lamb and Flávia Vieira

VOL. 16

Zu Qualitätssicherung und Peer Review der vorliegenden Publikation

Die Qualität der in dieser Reihe erscheinenden Arbeiten wird vor der Publikation durch Herausgeber der Reihe im Blind-Verfahren geprüft. Dabei ist der Autor der Arbeit den Gutachtern während der Prüfung namentlich nicht bekannt.

Notes on the quality assurance and peer review of this publication

Prior to publication, the quality of the work published in this series is blind reviewed by editors of the series. The referees are not aware of the author's name when performing their review.

Manuel Jiménez Raya / Terry Lamb / Flávia Vieira

Mapping Autonomy in Language Education

A Framework for Learner and Teacher Development

PETER LANG
EDITION

Bibliographic Information published by the Deutsche Nationalbibliothek
The Deutsche Nationalbibliothek lists this publication in the Deutsche Nationalbibliografie; detailed bibliographic data is available in the internet at http://dnb.d-nb.de.

Library of Congress Cataloging-in-Publication Data
A CIP catalog record for this book has been applied for at the Library of Congress

Cover image: © Flávia Manuela Ferreira Vieira

This publication has been sponsored by the Departamento de Filologías Inglesa y Alemana- University of Granada.

ISSN 1437-3157
ISBN 978-3-631-67360-7 (Print)
E-ISBN 978-3-631-72220-6 (E-PDF)
E-ISBN 978-3-631-72221-3 (EPUB)
E-ISBN 978-3-631-72222-0 (MOBI)
DOI 10.3726/b11095

© Peter Lang GmbH
Internationaler Verlag der Wissenschaften
Frankfurt am Main 2017
All rights reserved.
Peter Lang Edition is an Imprint of Peter Lang GmbH.

Peter Lang – Frankfurt am Main · Bern · Bruxelles · New York · Oxford · Warszawa · Wien

This publication has been peer reviewed.

www.peterlang.com

Table of contents

List of Tables

List of Figures

1. Introduction

> (...) human life will never be understood unless its highest aspirations are taken into account. Growth, self-actualization, the striving toward health, the quest for identity and autonomy, the yearning for excellence (and other ways of phrasing the striving upward) must now be accepted beyond question as a widespread and perhaps universal human tendency. (Maslow, 1970: xii–xiii)

The above ideas, expressed almost forty years ago, are just as relevant today. UNESCO's Declaration for Education 2030, which resulted from the World Education Forum 2015 in Incheon, clearly appeals to high human aspirations by endorsing a strategic vision that calls for *inclusive and equitable quality education and lifelong learning for all.* This Declaration "is inspired by a humanistic vision of education and development based on human rights and dignity; social justice; inclusion; protection; cultural, linguistic and ethnic diversity; and shared responsibility and accountability" (p. 7). Education is understood as a human right and a basis for guaranteeing peace, tolerance, human fulfilment, sustainable development, full employment, and the eradication of poverty. This is certainly an ambitious and essential vision, requiring that "teachers and educators are empowered, adequately recruited, well-trained, professionally qualified, motivated and supported within well-resourced, efficient and effectively governed systems" (p. 8).

In this book, our focus on pedagogy for autonomy in language education is also motivated by high aspirations, namely the enhancement of more democratic teaching and learning practices within a vision of (language) education in schools as a space for enacting (inter)personal empowerment and promoting social transformation. We are strongly convinced that the concept of "autonomy", which has long been researched and explored in many different ways, continues to be central in considerations of how education can become more inclusive and empowering for learners and teachers, particularly because educational systems have mostly served to reproduce and reinforce established educational and social traditions rather than transform them. In a radical manifesto against neoliberal, market-driven educational policies, Giroux points out the dangers of a 'pedagogy of repression' through which "students are conditioned to unlearn any respect for democracy, justice, and what it might mean to connect learning to social change", arguing that "this is a pedagogy that kills the spirit, promotes conformity, and is more suited to an authoritarian society than a democracy" (Giroux 2013, para. 15). As a result of the lack of democracy in educational settings, "millions of children leave school all over the world each day no better able to engage in democratic action and make changes in their communities to meet their needs than when they entered", and therefore we need to "construct curricula for challenge, for change, for the development of people and not the engineering of employees" (Schostak, 2000: 50). This appears to be a central justification for promoting pedagogy for autonomy in schools.

Generally speaking, autonomy refers to both a goal of education and a pedagogical approach to attaining that goal. The development of autonomy as an educational goal can be interpreted as "the development of a kind of person whose thought and action in important areas of his life are to be explained by reference to his own choices, decisions, reflections, deliberations—in short, his own activity of mind" (Dearden, 1972: 70). Additionally, autonomy is seen as crucial to the development of lifelong learning in 'the learning society'. Indeed, acting autonomously as a responsible, self-determined agent is fundamental for democratic citizenship and for moral decision-making in a world characterized by swift changes. Accordingly, a focus on autonomy in education is intrinsic to such significant values as democracy, liberty, justice, rights, and some versions of equality (Kerr, 2002). The concept of autonomy conveys the belief that all individuals, to some extent, have the right to participate in democratic life and to choose for themselves how to live their own lives. A democratic society is thus expected to foster the use of reason in social life and autonomy as an educational goal. The principle underlying the different perspectives on education as emancipation is the commitment to educational goals related to the Kantian idea of rational autonomy (Carr, 1996). According to Aviram & Yonah (2004), even current changes in the post-modern world that demand personal creativity, initiative, lifelong learning and independence make the notion of autonomy a valid goal for education.

Even though the explicit promotion of autonomy is largely absent from many school practices, it is present as a goal of language education in many European curricula (see Lamb, 2008; Jiménez Raya, 2011; Miliander, 2011; Trebbi, 2011; Vieira 2011). Furthermore the language policies set by the Council of Europe in the Common European Framework of Reference for Languages (Council of Europe, 2001a) stress the need to support the implementation of language teaching approaches that "strengthen independence of thought, judgement and action, combined with social skills and responsibility" (p. 4). In addition, autonomy has been the focus of research and experimentation for decades worldwide (Lamb, 2017) and learner autonomy is currently acknowledged as one of the main dimensions of foreign language education, as evidenced by Benson's (2016) contribution to a handbook on English Language Teaching edited by Hall (2016). It is important to note, however, that despite past and current developments, pedagogy for autonomy remains a marginal trend. For example, it is not mentioned in Howatt & Smith's (2014) historical account of English Language Teaching from a British and European perspective.

The main purpose of this book is to propose a framework for the development of learner and teacher autonomy in language education. The framework was first developed as one of the products of the project EuroPAL – *A European Pedagogy for Autonomous Learning – Educating Modern Language Teachers Through ICT*[1], on the basis of the premise that learner autonomy and teacher autonomy are closely interrelated in a school context and should be defined within a vision of education as empowerment and transformation. The first version of the framework, published in 2007 (Jiménez Raya, Lamb & Vieira, 2007)[2], was the basis for developing the present book by updating and expanding the initial one, which went out of circulation when the publisher closed. Our title – *Mapping Autonomy in Language Education – A Framework for Learner and Teacher Development* – stresses two metaphors used in the

---

1 EuroPAL was funded by the SOCRATES programme, action Comenius 2.1, and developed from October 2004 to October 2007 under the coordination of Manuel Jiménez Raya.
2 The authors were part of the EuroPAL team and were responsible for this first publication, although it was discussed with other team members: Charalambos Vrasidas, Michalinos Zembylas, Enrica Flamini, Ivan Shotlekov, June Miliander, and Turid Trebbi.

book. The "mapping" metaphor emphasises the need to bring forward the role of contexts, learners and teachers in shaping the ends and means of pedagogy for autonomy. Contexts, learners and teachers are understood as the structuring elements of a "framework" aimed at raising ethical, conceptual and practical issues that are crucial to our perspective and offer our readers a basis for reflection on learner and teacher development towards learner and teacher autonomy.

Throughout the book, our main concerns relate to *what makes pedagogy for autonomy distinctive:* What vision of education does it entail? What is the relationship between learner and teacher autonomy? What factors facilitate or hamper both? What learning and teaching competences are involved in pedagogy for autonomy? How might teachers enable it? What principles might guide their action? How can teacher education enhance pedagogy for autonomy? These kinds of question both orient our reasoning and proposals and inform teachers' local choices at the level of language teaching strategies and materials. In this way, we hope to help teachers consider the *rationale and implications* of pedagogy for autonomy so that their choices become more informed and critical.

The book is primarily directed at foreign language (prospective) teachers and teacher educators, although it may be of interest to other educational agents, especially school administrators, coursebook writers, and syllabus designers. By providing a comprehensive, flexible framework for the development of pedagogy for autonomy in school settings, we hope to promote critical reflection and purposeful, context-sensitive action towards the development of autonomy, favour comparative enquiry into pedagogical approaches in diverse language education contexts, and encourage a cross-disciplinary approach to autonomy issues. Although our concerns relate to language education in the school setting, we would like to stress the cross-disciplinary and cross-contextual potential of the book, which enhances its usefulness by encouraging a broad perspective on autonomy issues. Therefore, readers might wish to consider its applicability across different language and non-language pedagogical contexts, at different educational levels, and in various cultural settings.

Finally, it should be clear that although our proposal assumes a vision of education as empowerment and transformation, we have tried to integrate diverse theoretical contributions in the field, and our concern for comprehensiveness, context-sensitiveness and flexibility implies a fundamental respect for multiple voices in the educational community. Readers may identify with some ideas more than with others, and find some ideas more controversial than others; this is related both to the nature of their own personal theories, practices and professional contexts, as well as to the fact that any framework for the development of pedagogy for autonomy is necessarily exploratory and provisional, and therefore debatable.

2. Pedagogy for autonomy: underlying assumptions and general language teaching principles

In this section we focus on basic assumptions underlying pedagogy for autonomy and on the general language teaching principles that it should integrate. Before moving on, we would like to start with our definition of both learner and teacher autonomy, which will be further explained in chapter 3. We define *both* as...

> *The competence to develop as a self-determined, socially responsible and critically aware participant in (and beyond) educational environments, within a vision of education as (inter)personal empowerment and social transformation.*

This broad definition highlights *general aspects of autonomy and the vision of education it entails.* By having a common definition for learner and teacher autonomy, we want to stress their similar nature as well as their interdependence in school contexts. By adopting a subject-free definition, we wish to broaden its scope and underline its cross-disciplinary potential.

The assumptions behind our definition are briefly sketched in Figure 1 (see section 3.2.1 for a more detailed explanation as regards learner autonomy and 3.3.1 as regards teacher autonomy):

Figure 1. Definition of autonomy

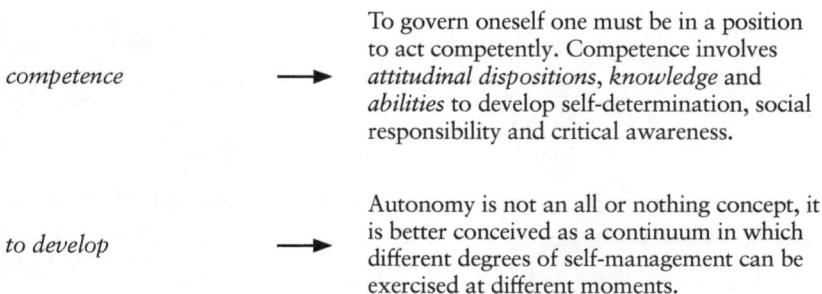

competence	$\longrightarrow$	To govern oneself one must be in a position to act competently. Competence involves *attitudinal dispositions, knowledge* and *abilities* to develop self-determination, social responsibility and critical awareness.
to develop	$\longrightarrow$	Autonomy is not an all or nothing concept, it is better conceived as a continuum in which different degrees of self-management can be exercised at different moments.

as a self-determined	→	Autonomy has an *individual dimension* (e.g. self-knowledge, responsible self-agency, self-regulation, self-direction).
socially responsible	→	Autonomy also has a *social dimension* (e.g. voice, respect for others, negotiation, co-operation, interdependence).
and critically aware	→	Autonomy has moral and political implications and involves the cultivation of an inquiring, independent mind.
participant	→	Autonomy involves assuming a *proactive* and *interactive* role.
in (and beyond) educational environments	→	Formal educational settings can and should allow individuals to exercise the right to develop autonomy and thus promote lifelong learning, which may occur both within and outside of an educational institution.
within a vision of education as (inter)personal empowerment and social transformation	→	Learner and teacher development towards autonomy assumes that education is a moral and political phenomenon whose goal is to transform (rather than reproduce) the *status quo*. In this sense, autonomy is a collective interest oriented by democratic and emancipatory ideals.

Bearing in mind the above definition, we now present the major assumptions underlying our view of pedagogy for autonomy.

2.1 Pedagogy for autonomy: major assumptions

Five assumptions are presented which help us build a general understanding of pedagogy for autonomy as we see it:

Pedagogy deals with the particular, the practical, and the possible
Pedagogy for autonomy is educationally and socially relevant
There cannot be a unified approach to pedagogy for autonomy
Pedagogy for autonomy is much more than a teaching methodology
Pedagogy for autonomy is not language-specific

Pedagogy deals with the particular, the practical, and the possible

Pedagogy is concerned with the ethical, conceptual and practical issues involved in the art and science of teaching to enhance learning. Kumaravadivelu (2001) argues that a postmodern pedagogy is a three-dimensional system consisting of three pedagogic parameters: *particularity*, *practicality*, and *possibility*. A pedagogy of particularity is context-sensitive and location-specific and therefore rejects the idea that it is possible to prescribe a common set of pedagogic aims and objectives that can be attained through one set of pedagogic principles and procedures. A pedagogy of practicality pertains to the relationship between theory and practice, and rejects the view of teachers as implementers of pre-defined knowledge or discourse (Giroux, 1988). It tries to overcome some of the deficiencies inherent in the dichotomies between theory and practice and between theorists' theory and teachers' theory by encouraging and enabling teachers to theorize from their practice and to practise what they theorize (Kumaravadivelu, 1999). A pedagogy of possibility is derived principally from Freire's (1994, 1996) educational philosophy and seeks to tap into the socio-political consciousness that learners and teachers bring with them to the foreign language classroom. The idea is that this can serve as a catalyst for social transformation and can help both teachers and learners in their quest for identity formation.

If we accept the validity of the pedagogic parameters of particularity, practicality, and possibility for the development of a pedagogy for autonomy, then we need a framework that is *comprehensive, context-sensitive and flexible*. This means that our proposal should attempt to integrate diverse contributions, should be interpreted through and confronted by other perspectives, and should instigate critical reflection rather than compliance.

Pedagogy for autonomy is educationally and socially relevant

Why should we develop pedagogy for autonomy? A basic reason lies perhaps in our *human disposition and need* to become self-determined individuals and active participants in social communities. From an ethical and political perspective, pedagogy for autonomy can also be a strategic endeavour in the *pursuit of democracy* in education and society at large. In addition, a substantial body of research (see Benson's review, 2011) confirms the existence of strong evidence indicating that controlling learning environments contribute to low achievement, anxiety, preference for easy work, and dependence on others to evaluate their work. Similarly, significant relationships have been found between the development of learner autonomy and a number of positive *learning gains* such as a sense of enjoyment and vitality, intrinsic motivation, increased perceived competence, preference for optimally difficult work, striving for conceptual understanding, critical awareness of learning processes, cooperative attitudes, decision-making abilities, and willingness to learn (see Deci & Ryan, 1987; Boggiano & Katz, 1991); such gains can contribute significantly to making language learning more meaningful, purposeful and accessible to all learners. Finally, pedagogy for autonomy implies that teachers become agents of change, so one of the main reasons for promoting it is that it favours *teacher empowerment* as well. Although this aspect of pedagogy for autonomy has often been ignored or perceived as a side effect, it is our contention that the development of learner autonomy is linked to reflective teacher development and can foster teachers' willingness and ability to challenge the *status quo* and to struggle for better educational and social conditions.

There cannot be a unified approach to pedagogy for autonomy

The complexity of the notion of autonomy makes it clear that pedagogy for autonomy does not lend itself to being expressed in a straightforward, univocal manner. The literature on learner autonomy reveals a number of overviews of the meaning and history of and research into autonomy in language learning (see Benson's review, 2011). Reading this literature, it is clear that definitions of learner autonomy are problematic, the reason being that it manifests itself in multifarious ways, depending on the context in which it is found, the purposes and principles which underpin it, and the broader philosophical, ideological, political, cultural, social and educational influences which are at play. Given such multidimensionality, as well as its relationship to related fields of research, such as learner-centredness (Nunan, 1988; Tudor, 1996) and experiential learning (Kohonen et al., 2001), it is no wonder, then, that the literature on learner autonomy encompasses many diverse fields and is interpreted in diverse ways. This is exemplified in the research strand investigating learner autonomy (and its validity) in different cultural contexts, and the insights into different representations of autonomy, which such research offers.

At a practical level we also find a great diversity of local understandings and methodological frameworks which may focus on different aspects of learner autonomy, some of which have been developed as part of communicative language teaching (e.g. project work, task-based learning, flexible independent learning, self-access learning, learner training, cooperative learning, negotiated/process syllabus, language portfolio, etc.). However, we must bear in mind that autonomy is not a matter of all or nothing. At any rate, learner-control – which is an essential component of autonomous learning – is not a single, unitary concept, but rather a continuum along which various learning situations may be placed. There are degrees of student involvement that the individual teacher can facilitate, taking into consideration not only the amount of responsibility s/he is prepared and able to share and the amount of responsibility learners are prepared and able to assume, but also the contextual circumstances of teaching and learning. This implies that learner and teacher roles have to be constantly negotiated and redefined as pedagogy for autonomy evolves.

Rather than being constrained by definitions, then, we must remain sensitive and open to individual circumstances and contexts. The contextual nature of autonomy suggests that it can be construed in many different ways, and that we must follow the scent rather than look for the specific, adopting a *critical analytical approach* in order to understand what is happening (or not) and why. The view we present in this book is intended to encourage such an approach.

Pedagogy for autonomy is much more than a teaching methodology

Although pedagogy for autonomy can take various forms, it is our belief that it should refer to a vision of education as *empowerment* and *transformation* rather than oppression and reproduction. This means that learners and teachers are seen as critical (rather than passive) consumers and creative producers of knowledge, co-managers of teaching and learning processes, and partners in pedagogical negotiation; it also means abandoning a reified notion of knowledge in favour of a view of knowledge as a dynamic construct of the knower (teacher and learner); finally, it means that education is seen as an opportunity to struggle for a better life, that is, life that is more rational, just and satisfactory.

Therefore, pedagogy for autonomy is much more than a teaching methodology. Commitment to autonomy depends largely on one's *ideological options* as a person and as a teacher. It implies an *emancipatory view of teaching and of the teacher's role* in society, thus refusing the view that schools are institutions designed only to reproduce an outside fixed social structure and that no teacher can be empowered to exert any influence on social reconstruction.

It also implies *accepting the uncertainty and difficulty of innovative pedagogical action*, as well as a *critical stance towards constraints* on teacher and learner empowerment (Lamb, 2000a; Jiménez Raya, 2017; Vieira, 1997, 1998, 2003, 2009).

Pedagogy for autonomy is not language-specific

Autonomy has been broadly recognized as a fundamental value in moral and political philosophy (Callan, 1988; Dworkin, 1988; Guyer, 2003; Lindley, 1986), occupying a prominent position in theoretical accounts of persons, conceptions of moral obligation and responsibility, social policies and many other areas of political theory. The notion of learner autonomy as an educational goal pervades school curricula worldwide.

This is the reason why our approach in this book assumes our belief in the *cross-disciplinary value of autonomy as an educational goal*. This means that our pedagogical reasoning moves beyond the particularities of language teaching and learning to embrace broader issues that will be of interest to any teacher and teacher educator. We do not see this as a weakness of our framework. As a matter of fact, we would argue that keeping the debate of pedagogy for autonomy within the boundaries of language-specific aspects may serve to de-politicize our views of what pedagogy for autonomy in language education entails, in particular by removing it from the larger arena of schooling and its relationship with society. We would further contend that language teachers who are interested in developing pedagogy for autonomy should become critical inquirers of the political and moral nature and impact of school pedagogy, and work collaboratively with teachers of other subjects in their educational communities. Ultimately then, developing pedagogy for autonomy entails a *whole-school project for learner and teacher development.*

2.2 Pedagogy for autonomy and general language teaching principles

Even though we advocate a cross-disciplinary view of autonomy as an educational goal, pedagogy for autonomy in language education must necessarily integrate general language teaching principles that emerge from theory and research on second language acquisition and language teaching methodology.

Any modern language teaching proposal must necessarily tackle some of the most controversial issues in language teaching methodology. These issues deal with the nature of foreign language competence, the role played by intercultural learning in language education, the importance of catering to individual differences in learners, the contributions of both focus on meaning and focus on form, the role of both implicit and explicit second language knowledge, the problems posed by the learner's 'internal syllabus', and the roles of input, output and interaction in modern language learning. A theory of language teaching seeks to capture all those components, plus whatever else can be done to make modern language teaching efficient and effective.

The language education principles proposed below represent a variety of perspectives and are offered as a set of working 'specifications' for modern language pedagogy, the main reason for this being the fact that Second Language Acquisition (SLA) and Foreign Language Teaching methodology still cannot provide definite answers to some of the most controversial issues in language teaching. Therefore, any principles must be applied with caution and with reference to contexts. However, various disciplines have provided the theoretical bases from which to derive informed insights for language teaching. Accordingly, language teaching methodology should, as far as possible:

Create a natural language learning environment
Treat language holistically
Focus on both implicit and explicit knowledge
Focus on both meaning and form
Create an acquisition rich classroom

Take into consideration the learners' 'internal syllabus'
Provide error feedback
Promote intercultural competence

Creating a natural language learning environment

In the real world, language use is something natural. However, in many language classrooms language learning can still be described using the words Rivers used three decades ago: "a tedious, dry-as-dust process" (Rivers, 1987: 11) with its focus on accuracy and grammar practice. Language learners need opportunities to experience authentic use, especially because exposure to the target language in schools is limited and the effects of formal language instruction are also limited (Ortega, 2009).

In order to create a natural language learning environment, the following should be observed (Hughes 2001: 19): language skills integration; language which is contextualised; language relating directly to the learner; language which is linked to immediate and visible action; language which is both verbal and non-verbal; language which is meaningfully repeated on a daily basis; language which is extensive in quantity and occurs over an extended period of time. The extensive use of the target language in the classroom helps learners acquire it more efficiently, although there may be situations, for example with low-achieving learners, where the intentional use of the learners' mother-tongue can facilitate the development of certain competences, especially as regards language and learning awareness.

Treating language holistically

One of the first issues one encounters when discussing the role of instruction in language learning concerns the division of language into smaller parts for teaching. This is the issue of part vs. whole training discussed in the literature (see Johnson, 1995; Stern, 1992). Should we attempt to divide language up into pieces for instructional purposes? In language teaching the part/whole debate has tended to be argued in terms of extreme positions. As opposed to an approach which reduces language to tiny parts because it is easier to teach them, we advocate a holistic approach. The purpose is to avoid breaking down language into the smallest possible parts. This way we avoid what some authors have called the 'decomposition fallacy' which argues that breaking language down into simpler components does not always make it easier for students. As pointed out by Pearson & Raphael (1990: 234), "The danger is that the component sub-skills, which the curriculum designer may have conceptualized as mere stepping stones (enabling skills) on the way to complex skill mastery, become ends unto themselves". In addition, research shows that individuals do not learn isolated items in the target language one at a time, in an additive, linear fashion, but rather as parts of complex mappings of form-function relationships. Acquisition does entail the mastery of forms but of form-meaning mappings that are subject to ongoing revision as new forms are incorporated in the interlanguage system (Ellis & Shintani, 2014). Therefore, language learners need to experience language in its full complexity. From our perspective, the classroom should be conceived of as a unique social environment, in which teachers need to foster rich learning experiences which generate realistically motivated communication, allowing learners to speak for themselves, create authentic texts, and find solutions to relevant issues and problems. Task-based language teaching, for example, with its primary emphasis on meaning and communication reflects a holistic view of learning.

Focusing on both implicit and explicit knowledge

Current SLA theory asserts that instruction needs to be directed at developing both implicit and explicit knowledge, giving priority to the former, because as Ellis (2005: 306) has stated, "the bulk of language acquisition is implicit learning from usage. Most knowledge is tacit knowledge; most learning is implicit". Furthermore, it is the sole basis for spontaneous performance and is unaffected by instruction (Schmidt, 1995). In addition, there appears to be no direct link between the rules of grammar (as explicitly learnt), the explicit processing of language and the implicit tallying that makes possible the construction of linguistic competence (Paradis, 2009).

Implicit knowledge is procedural. Procedural knowledge is accessed rapidly and easily and it is available for use in fluent communication. Therefore, it is implicit knowledge that should constitute the goal of language learning. Implicit language learning can be characterized as incidental, involving some degree of attention to linguistic forms in the input (although there is controversy regarding the degree to which this attention is conscious) but not involving any depth of awareness regarding the abstract system that underlies the forms which have been attended to and internalized.

Even though competence in a foreign language seems to be primarily a matter of implicit knowledge, explicit knowledge can contribute to language and communication awareness. However, teachers should not assume that explicit knowledge, that is, declarative knowledge of the phonological, lexical, grammatical, pragmatic and socio-cultural features of language (Ellis, 2004), can automatically be converted into implicit knowledge, as the extent to which this is possible remains controversial. According to Paradis (2004), implicit linguistic competence and metalinguistic knowledge are different as evidence found in neurofunctional, neurophysiological and neuroanatomical research studies on bilinguals using neuroimaging techniques has confirmed. These two types of knowledge have different memory sources (declarative vs. procedural) and "implicit competence and explicit knowledge coexist. Neither one becomes the other" (Paradis 2004: 61).

Good language learners (see Naiman et al., 1978; Rubin, 1975) nevertheless seem to pay conscious attention to grammar and to learning a large number of rules. Explicit learning is necessarily intentional. It requires learners' conscious attention to the formal properties of the input, possibly at the expense of attending to meaning. Alternatively, explicit learning requires learners to spot elements in their implicit knowledge and reflect on them. Irrespective of whether explicit knowledge is derived from input or from earlier acquired implicit knowledge, it involves an attempt to construct rules or generalizations of which the learners will have a high level of awareness. According to Bialystok (1994), explicit knowledge is knowledge that includes precise boundaries and is organised in known systems. This knowledge may assist language development by facilitating the development of implicit knowledge.

It can be seen that different theoretical positions (DeKeyser, 1998; Krashen, 1981; Paradis, 2004, 2009; VanPatten & Williams, 2006) hold different views as to the value and contribution to second language acquisition of these two types of knowledge. However, the majority of researchers maintain that language acquisition is mostly an implicit task. There is a general agreement on the need to create opportunities for communicative activity in the classroom to develop implicit knowledge. For this reason, communicative tasks should occupy a central position when the goal is the development of implicit knowledge. This is not intended to deny a role in language acquisition for explicit knowledge; in fact, it can contribute to the creation of implicit knowledge. Under this view, declarative (explicit/metalinguistic) knowledge linked to learning is learnt on the basis of explicit and conscious information, while procedural (implicit) knowledge related to acquisition develops as a result of unconscious and implicit information: "The two interact in language comprehension and production but grow independently" (Towell, 2013: 126).

Focusing on both meaning and form

There is now a widespread acceptance that language acquisition requires that learners attend both to meaning and form. Indeed, according to some SLA theories, attention to form is necessary for acquisition to take place. Schmidt (1994), for example, has argued that there is no learning without conscious attention to form. For him, attention to form refers to the noticing of specific linguistic features, not awareness of grammatical rules. Recent developments tend to support a focus on form, that is, attention to form is to be embedded in the communicative interactions learners are involved in. Focus on form is defined in opposition to 'focus on forms'. A focus on form involves a focus on formal elements of language in the context of a communicative activity, while a focus on forms is restricted to such a focus. Probably the basic premise of focus-on-form instruction is that meaning and use have to be evident to the learner when his/her attention is drawn to the formal properties of language necessary to get the meaning across.

According to Ellis (2005), language instruction can encourage a focus on form in a number of ways:

- Through grammar activities designed to help learners acquire specific grammatical features by means of input- or output processing. This can use both inductive and deductive strategies.
- Through focused tasks. These are language learning tasks that aim at helping learners to comprehend and process specific grammatical structures in the input, and/or to produce the structures in the performance of the task.

- By means of methodological options that induce attention to form in the context of performing a communicative task: language awareness (James & Garret, 1991), consciousness raising (Rutherford, 1987), or input enhancement (Sharwood Smith, 1993).

We would wish to reiterate that focus on form should not be an end in itself, but, whichever approach is being taken, it should be with the intention of developing both implicit knowledge and communication. In other words, attention to meaning is even more central in the facilitation of language acquisition. A meaning-focused classroom seeks to involve learners in purposeful tasks which are embedded in meaningful contexts and which reflect and rehearse language as it is used authentically in the world outside the classroom. Meaning-focused instruction supplies the learner with input for processing. It also provides opportunities for learner output, and this contributes to the acquisition of implicit knowledge (Ellis, 1990). Negotiation of meaning can be directed at either avoiding problems that could otherwise arise in conversations or correcting problems once they arise. A focus on meaning is of greater relevance for language acquisition. For this reason, language teaching should place a greater emphasis on the creation of opportunities for communication in the classroom.

Creating an acquisition rich classroom

Language learning, whether it occurs in a naturalistic or an instructed context, is an enormously complex task. Simplifying grammar, vocabulary and using shorter sentences results in a more limited source of target-language use upon which learners must rely in order to learn the language. In this task, input, output and interaction are essential components.

a) Input

The input available to second language learners "is the raw data from which they derive both meaning and awareness of the rules and structures of the target language" (Chaudron, 1985: 3). In instructed language acquisition, input is of special importance because it is amenable to external manipulation. Target language input can either be entirely naturalistic, enhanced or structured in some way in an endeavour to draw the learner's attention to a target form, to require learners to process a target language form more effectively, or both. Teachers can make adjustments to the kind of input that the learners experience. To ensure adequate access to the language, teachers need to maximise use of the target language in the classroom and encourage opportunities for language exposure outside the classroom. In addition, input should be:

- *Comprehensible.* The challenge for teaching is to make sure that the input learners have access to is indeed comprehensible. This can be done by providing non-linguistic means of encouraging comprehension. Comprehension is a necessary condition for language acquisition, but not sufficient.
- *Meaning-bearing* (Barcroft & Wong, 2013). Successful language acquisition involves the mapping of a vast number of linguistic forms onto their meanings (form-meaning connections or mapping). If the input provided is not meaning-bearing or sufficiently comprehensible, learners will not be able to map the form with its meaning.
- *Interesting and/or relevant.* Input should be related to situations and knowledge that are connected to learners' interests, needs and background experience, so as to engage them and promote meaningful learning.
- *Not grammatically sequenced.* Grammatically-based syllabi reduce the quality of comprehensible input and distort the communicative focus. One of the assumptions that underlies the linguistic grading of items in a structural syllabus is that some items are easier to learn than others. Nonetheless, the criteria that have been used to grade items lack precision and there is no fixed procedure for determining the optimal language teaching sequence.
- *Sufficient in quantity.* Too much or too little input, particularly as regards contact with new language items, can affect learning, in the first case by increasing learning difficulty and in the second case by reducing learning challenge. The amount of input must take into account the learners' competence and maturity, as well as the learning goals set by the teacher.
- *Elaborated.* Both authentic and simplified texts may be inappropriate for certain learners from a psycholinguistic perspective. It is argued that authentic texts are too complex for learners and therefore need explicit metalinguistic study to make them comprehensible, which leads, in turn,

to the study of language as an object rather than the development of a functional ability to use language. *Elaboration* is the term given to the multitude of ways native speakers modify discourse to make meaning comprehensible. Most of the modifications occur during negotiation for meaning. Since elaborated texts do this while keeping the new lexical and grammatical items which learners need to encounter in the input, while preserving the semantic content of the genuine version (Long & Ross, 1993), and while presenting target language samples that are closer to authentic target language use than simplified versions, elaboration is clearly superior to simplification as a way of modifying input for foreign language learners. This does not, however, imply that we question the use of authentic texts. This would contradict the above principle advocating a holistic treatment of language.

ICT developments have made access to input really easy. Teachers should take advantage of these and explore ways in which learners can be exposed through them to target language input, thus extending learning beyond the classroom.

b) Output

In addition to input, it is also accepted that output plays a crucial role in the process of learning a second or foreign language. It is absolutely essential that learners are encouraged to experiment with and play with language. The process of experimentation will give rise to numerous mistakes along the way. Teachers need to admit that mistakes are part of an active and creative process of language construction. What looks like a mistake can in fact be a sign of progress. Swain (1995) summarizes the contributions that output can make:

- Production serves to generate better input through the feedback that learners' efforts at production elicit;
- It forces syntactic processing (i.e. obliges learners to pay attention to grammar);
- It allows learners to test out hypotheses about the target language grammar;
- It helps to automatize existing knowledge;

- It provides opportunities for learners to develop discourse skills, for example by producing *long turns*;
- It is important for helping learners to develop a *personal voice* by steering conversation on to topics they are interested in contributing to.

Furthermore, output provides the learner with *auto-input* (i.e. learners can attend to the input provided by their own productions) (Ellis, 2003).

c) Interaction

If input and output are important in language acquisition, so is their co-occurrence in oral interaction. We can distinguish between interactional and non-interactional input. Interactional input tends to be more comprehensible because it allows for negotiation of meaning. Non-interactional input is more challenging for the learner because there is no negotiation of meaning. Long (1983), for instance, has argued that allowing learners to negotiate for meaning whenever a communication problem arises promotes acquisition. It has been hypothesized that the comprehensible input that results from input modifications and, in particular, from interactional modifications facilitates the natural development of a second language. Interactional modifications create new resources, provide corrective feedback, and push learners to modify their own output. Johnson (1995) identifies four key requirements for interaction to create an acquisition-rich classroom: creating contexts of language use where students have a reason to attend to language; providing opportunities for learners to use the language to express their own personal meanings; helping students to participate in language-related activities that are beyond their current level of proficiency; and encouraging them to participate in a full range of contexts that cater for a full performance in the language.

Taking into consideration the learners' 'internal syllabus'

As shown by early research into naturalistic SLA, the idea that what teachers teach is what learners learn, and when they teach it is when learners learn it, is not only simplistic, but wrong. Acquisition sequences do not mirror teaching sequences, and *teachability* is constrained by *learnability* (Pienemann, 1984). In the SLA literature, we can find strong evidence for different kinds of developmental sequences and stages in interlanguage development, such as the six-stage sequence for English relative clauses (Doughty, 1991); the four-stage sequence for ESL negation (Pica, 1983), and many other grammatical areas. These sequences cannot be altered by teaching, in the sense that it is impossible to make learners skip stages or alter them altogether (Ellis, 1989). Research has, nonetheless, demonstrated that teaching can help learners speed up passage through the sequences and in general help them improve accuracy, rate of learning, and level of ultimate attainment (Doughty, 2003; Long, 1988).

Teaching should avoid useless attempts to impose an external linguistic syllabus on learners, and instead, provide conditions for input that is at least roughly tuned to learners' current processing capacity. Doughty & Long (2003) argue that task-based language teaching is particularly suitable. In task-based teaching, language is never the primary focus of instruction.

Providing error feedback

Evidence from SLA research suggests that error feedback can be effective, if it is sustained over an extended period of time, and focused on something that the learners are actually capable of learning. The necessity of negative feedback for language learning remains a controversial issue. Work on both traditional explicit teacher error correction and implicit negative feedback in the form of corrective recasts (Braidi, 2002; DeKeyser, 1993) suggests strongly that negative feedback can be facilitative, at the very least, with certain classes of language structures. *Recasts* involve the reformulation of all or part of a student's utterance. They are proposed as an effective (but not the only) form of negative feedback in task-based language teaching for certain classes of grammatical and lexical problems, because they are not intrusive on the processing of meaning while learners are accomplishing a task and do not depend upon metalinguistic discussion of a language problem. In fact, what has been described as "negative feedback" can become a "positive interactional strategy" as long as it encourages learners to address their learning problems in a way that does not decrease their self-confidence and willingness to learn.

For Johnson (1988, 1996) the error/mistake distinction is a manifestation of the more general knowledge/processing ability distinction. Based on the assumption that the literature on language acquisition has paid more attention to errors than mistakes, he discusses the eradication of mistakes (i.e. learners' failure to perform a task) in terms of the literature on skill acquisition and maintains that "learners need to see for themselves what has gone wrong, in the operating conditions under which they went wrong" (Johnson, 1988: 93). Johnson suggests that the kind of practice that is most liable to lead to increased accuracy will involve the stages of corrective action and retrial. He argues that the most effective way to correct mistakes is best executed not by means of formal explanation but by "confronting the learner with the mismatch between flawed and model performance" (ibid.: 93) and that the latter entails opportunities for performing the skill in free practice (i.e. practice that corresponds to the type of language use that the learner is trying to master). One way in which this takes place is when learners receive requests to clarify utterances that contain linguistic errors (Pica et al., 1989).

Fostering the development of intercultural competence

Advances in sociolinguistics (e.g. Hymes, 1972), schema learning theory (e.g. Bartlett, 1932) and pragmatics (e.g. Brown, 1994) have exerted a decisive influence on our understanding of the role culture plays on communication in intercultural contexts and the need to incorporate the cultural dimension in language teaching practice. It is generally agreed that without opportunities to acquire the complex system of cultural customs, values, and ways of thinking, feeling and acting that pervade a language, learners will be severely limited in their attempts to use the language communicatively (Brown, 1994; Kaikkonen, 2001; Kramsch, 1993). Byram & Zarate (1994) have suggested that foreign language learners, rather than trying to approximate the native speaker, should be taught instead how to become intercultural speakers. The aim would be to help learners analyse, reflect upon and interpret foreign cultural phenomena when using the language in contact with foreign nationals. The teacher's responsibility is to teach culture as it is mediated through language, so as to increase pupils' knowledge and understanding of the relevant culture, break down prejudice among pupils and develop pupils' ability to see similarities and differences between countries (Byram & Risager, 1999). Fostering intercultural competence provides a background and context which brings the speech community to life, and helps the student to visualize and vicariously experience that reality (Stern, 1992). According to Beacco et al. (2010: 8), intercultural dialogue "makes it easier to understand otherness, to make cognitive and affective connections between past and new experiences of otherness, mediate between members of two (or more) social groups and their cultures, and question the assumptions of one's own cultural group and environment". Intercultural skills and know-how include cultural awareness and sensitivity, the ability to establish relations and mediate between cultures, and the ability to overcome intercultural misunderstandings and stereotyped relationships (Council of Europe, 2001a: 104–105).

Our assumption that the general language teaching principles proposed above should be integrated into pedagogy for autonomy in language education suggests that promoting this kind of pedagogy in schools does *not* mean breaking away from what has been called "communicative language teaching". It does suggest, however, that a communicative approach is not sufficient to promote learner autonomy, especially in terms of the development of learning awareness, strategic learning, participation in decision-making, and a critical view of (language) education (see Vieira, 1998: 67–68). It also suggests that we have to find new ways of integrating the lessons we have learnt from research, as our commitments demand a critical and radical rethink about teacher and learner roles. In other words, the theories above do not incorporate and problematize the implications of schooling for (inter)personal empowerment and social transformation.

3. Mapping pedagogy for autonomy

A vision of education as empowerment and transformation necessarily interrogates the role of contexts, learners and teachers in shaping the ends and means of pedagogy. *Mapping pedagogy for autonomy* is the metaphor we use to emphasize that role by bringing forward elements that may foster or constrain learner and teacher development. This will provide the background for defining a set of pedagogical principles in chapter 4.

3.1 Putting the context on the map

Analysing the context in which a pedagogy for autonomy may develop requires levels of analysis ranging from the social and ideological to the psychological, and this becomes even more complex when looking at different European institutions where the importance which might be placed on these different levels of analysis is difficult to predict. What is needed is a conceptual framework which enables teachers and teacher educators to make comparative analyses and provides guidance for them in understanding and developing their own context-specific work.

One way of conceptualising such a framework is to draw a distinction between the *conditions* which may allow pedagogy for autonomy to develop (or indeed constrain it) and the *forces* which may drive (or constrain) this development. In other words, it is useful to distinguish between the local, national and international setting or context in which language learning and teaching operates, and the drivers or constraints which either propel or restrict the development of learner autonomy. By locating themselves in this landscape and understanding the conditions which obtain and the forces which sweep across it, teachers can consider critically their location within it and find ways of navigating through it, either removing the constraints or working round them, in any case *exploiting their professional context in ways which will move them forward rather than hold them back.*

The purpose of this section is to attempt to identify the elements which make up this landscape, exploring not only the setting but also the forces which blow across it, and the dynamic interplay between these forces.

3.1.1 Understanding the setting

The setting in which a teacher teaches and a learner learns extends beyond the confines of the school. It extends to the broad socio-economic and cultural contexts which shape the demands made on the education system. It encompasses the dominant structures which surround and permeate the education system, and the policy frameworks (local, national, international) in which they operate. It also includes the professional ideologies and experiences of the teachers and teacher educators as well as the beliefs about learning held by the learners, and the experiential background which shapes those beliefs. Such settings have themselves evolved over time and have been subjected to historical forces which have served to embed particular principles, purposes and practices within them; this evolution has led to a situation in which *structurally the setting is conducive to or antagonistic towards a pedagogy for autonomy* (or paradoxically, and perhaps most often, both conducive and antagonistic).

The setting involves a complex set of conditions in which teachers and learners operate. The following list is an attempt to categorise these conditions, though it must be stressed that there will inevitably be overlaps between the categories. As you read them, we invite you to consider the following questions in relation to your own context: *What form(s) do these conditions take in my context? To what extent do they facilitate or hinder the development of pedagogy for autonomy? What spaces for manoeuvre can be created and how?* You may use Table 1 below to identify constraints and transformation strategies.

- *Dominant ideological/political/sociocultural/economic/educational values* (e.g. social and economic cooperation/competitiveness, inclusion/exclusion, collaboration/individualism, open-mindedness/xenophobia, progressivism/conservatism, transformation and emancipation/social and cultural reproduction, resistance/resignation, criticality/obedience to authority, etc.)
- *Dominant traditions, frameworks and guidelines in language teaching and learning* (e.g. methodologies promoted by educational policies, national curricula and assessment systems, textbooks and other resources, teacher education curricula, teacher competences, etc.)

- *Dominant family and/or community expectations* (e.g. as regards teacher/learner roles, educational aspirations, importance of language learning, assessment criteria, etc.)
- *Dominant institutional "culture" and demands* (e.g. as regards management structures, ethos, democracy, student voice, regulations, inspection, curriculum, coverage of syllabus, teaching and learning policy, examinations, certification, time and space organization, number of students per class, resources, etc.)
- *Dominant teacher education (pre/in-service) discourses and practices* (e.g. applicationist/reflective paradigms, centralised/localised policies, relationships between theory and practice, university/school involvement, evaluation agendas, teacher voice, etc.)
- *Teachers' past experience as learners* (e.g. teacher/learner-dominated, democratic/ inclusive/ authoritarian, etc.)
- *Teachers' language teaching experiences* (e.g. teacher/learner-centred, reflective/unreflective, engaged/conformist, monolingual/multilingual contexts, learner motivation, which language, etc.)
- *Teachers' personal theories (values, attitudes, beliefs, knowledge)* (as regards language teaching and learning e.g. metacognitive knowledge, teacher/learner roles, methodology, assessment, inclusion/exclusion of all learners, homogeneous/heterogeneous classrooms, etc.)
- *Teachers' sociocultural / linguistic background* (e.g. country of origin, teaching first/second/third language, cultural experiences of language being taught, residence abroad, etc.)
- *Teachers' professional values* (e.g. professionally engaged/professionally demotivated, commitment to collegiality/individualism and detachment, teacher as learner/"fossilization", professional commitment/absenteeism, etc.)
- *Learners' past learning experience, including language learning experiences* (e.g. teacher/learner-directed, democratic/inclusive/authoritarian, exposure to other languages, etc.)
- *Learners' personal theories (values, attitudes, beliefs, knowledge) as regards language teaching and learning* (e.g. metacognitive knowledge, teacher/learner roles, methodology, assessment, etc.)
- *Learners' sociocultural/linguistic background* (e.g. parental background, bilingual/multilingual background, experiences of other cultures, etc.)

- *Learners' commitment to education and lifelong learning* (e.g. socioeconomic status, sense of relevance and relatedness regarding school culture and curriculum, motivation/disaffection towards school, compliance or positive resistance/disruptiveness or absenteeism, achievement/underachievement, active engagement/passivity, etc.)

Table 1. Reflection on constraints to pedagogy for autonomy and transformation strategies

Consider the conditions that may foster or hinder pedagogy for autonomy and identify specific constraints that you consider to be <u>most influential</u> in your own situation. Discuss your opinions with other colleagues if possible. Make notes on the "transformation strategies" column.

Social and educational aspects		
The setting	Constraints to promoting pedagogy for autonomy	Transformation Strategies (What can be done)
1. Dominant ideological/ political/ sociocultural/ economic/ educational values 2. Dominant traditions, frameworks and guidelines in language teaching and learning 3. Dominant family and/ or community expectations 4. Dominant institutional "culture" and demands		

Teacher related aspects		
The setting	Constraints to promoting pedagogy for autonomy	Transformation Strategies (What can be done)
5. Dominant teacher education (pre/in-service) discourses and practices 6. Teachers' past experience as learners 7. Teachers' language teaching experiences		

Teacher related aspects		
The setting	Constraints to promoting pedagogy for autonomy	Transformation Strategies (What can be done)
8. Teachers' personal theories 9. Teachers' sociocultural / linguistic background 10. Teachers' professional values		

Learner related aspects		
The setting	Constraints to promoting pedagogy for autonomy	Transformation Strategies (What can be done)
11. Learners' past learning experience, including language learning experiences 12. Learners' personal theories 13. Learners' sociocultural/ linguistic background 14. Learners' commitment to education and lifelong learning		

Other constraints (specify):	

No matter how favourable or unfavourable to pedagogy for autonomy the above conditions are in particular contexts, no teacher is either totally context-free or totally context-bound. Moreover, the possibility of developing learner autonomy seems to be largely dependent on *how teachers perceive these conditions*, perhaps more than on the conditions themselves: in the same context, different teachers can reason and act differently, even radically differently (see Lamb, 1998, 2000a, for an example of how some teachers could interpret a new and prescriptive national curriculum in such a way as to justify the development of flexible learning, when its impact on other teachers was to discourage innovation).

3.1.2 Understanding the propelling and constraining forces

The forces which propel or constrain the development of a pedagogy for autonomy across this landscape may not only be historical but also current and contemporaneous with teacher and learner development. They are a complex mixture of forces, which can range from those that are local in origin to those that result from globalisation processes. Two major examples of the latter as regards language education policies and practices in Europe can be found in the Common European Framework of Reference for Languages (Council of Europe, 2001a) and the European Language Portfolio (ELP, Council of Europe, 2001b), both proposed as a means to foster plurilingualism and pluriculturalism, as well as communication, mobility and co-operation among European countries towards the development of democratic citizenship.

As you read the following attempt to categorise the forces which may propel or constrain the development of a pedagogy for autonomy, you can ask yourself the following questions: *How are these driving forces impacting on the context in which I work? Where are they coming from? What implications are there for the development of autonomy?*

1. *Theoretical.* The development of learner autonomy has gained impetus from theories as diverse as communicative language teaching, learner-centredness, (social-)constructivism, and democracy in the classroom, as well as theories about the role of education and discussions focused around the relative importance of content and process. However, theory is not always developed in conjunction with practice, which means that its impact on teachers and learners is sometimes limited. Valuing teacher experience and enquiry more systematically seems to be a requisite for further developments in the field.
2. *Professional.* Shifts within the concept of 'effective' teaching and learning, the role of the teacher (and the teacher educator), reflective practice, professionalism, and (in some contexts) the demand for compliance to increasing government control over teacher training and professional development (Lamb & Simpson, 2003) and school inspection/quality

assurance regimes have influenced in both qualitative and substantive ways teachers' willingness, ability and freedom to innovate, let alone to encourage increased learner autonomy. In some contexts, teacher education curricula are transmissive and application-oriented, which prevents teachers and teachers-to-be from assuming a more active role in the construction of pedagogical knowledge and the transformation of school practices.

3. *Practical.* Pedagogical enquiry undertaken all over the world by researchers and practitioners has shown that pedagogy can promote learner autonomy in various aspects (metacognitive awareness, strategic learning, ability to negotiate, make decisions and self-evaluate, critical stance towards learning and teaching, etc.), thus validating pedagogy for autonomy from a practical, as well as theoretical, perspective (i.e. it works!); but it also points out the diversity and fragmentation of approaches and the need to constantly scrutinise their transformative value.

4. *Political.* From the micro-politics of the school to the macro-politics of central governments and European institutions, the development of (a pedagogy for) autonomy has been embroiled in political debate both large and small, e.g. on issues related to the neoliberal agenda, social justice and inclusion, voice and influence, education for, access to and promotion of citizenship, plurilingualism and pluriculturalism, European mobility etc. Furthermore, the trend in many contexts towards centralised policies with regard to school management, curricula and quality control, as well as the growth of transnational policies regarding standardised assessment and accountability (see Smith, 2016), tend to normalise schooling rather than promote its role in social change.

5. *Economic.* From encouragement of learner autonomy as a means to developing entrepreneurism and economic success to introduction of self-access learning as a way of making cuts in the teaching force, economic forces impact on the development of learner autonomy and may reduce its value for (inter)personal growth, through legitimising an instrumental view of education.

6. *Technological.* The increase in technological capacity to support learning has led to new forms of learning, e.g. e-/b-learning, self-access learning etc., and with these, new roles for the learner, but it also has the potential to exclude those learning in technology-poor contexts or those with

limited experience of or confidence in the use of technology. Furthermore, there appears to be an assumption that the application of some technologies *per se* means that learners are learning autonomously, and that this is the intention of such developments, despite evidence that in some cases the machine is simply replacing a teacher-centred classroom, or indeed being used to make economies in teaching staff (Lamb, 2005a).

Some of the above factors are rather insidious and not always open to public debate, thus constituting a kind of "hidden agenda" that needs to be made explicit and scrutinised. Moreover, as conflicting factors often co-exist, it may be difficult to understand which interests are being served by a particular theory, policy or practice. *Who benefits from what* may not always be clear, but asking this question is a moral responsibility of any educator. A good example is perhaps the European Language Portfolio, whose pedagogical function to promote reflective and autonomous learning, self-assessment and appreciation of linguistic and cultural diversity can be challenged by its informative function to measure, record and formally recognise language attainment on the basis of a unified set of performance descriptors. This kind of tension can be found in any pedagogical situation that combines formative and summative purposes. Actually, this is the case with schooling in general, and pedagogy for autonomy within schools is no exception.

3.1.3 Moving forward through the landscape

It is to be hoped that, by reflecting on the issues raised in the previous two sections, a way of understanding the setting and forces which define your context has emerged, which will enable you to move forward in the development of a pedagogy for autonomy. However, in order to do so, it is important to recognise that the nature of the interrelationship between the forces and the setting is itself complex, but that this also offers opportunities to develop such a pedagogy. It is *not* a story of static background subjected to a series of dynamic forces. The setting itself is dynamic, and produces additional forces which can both provide resistance and sources of support for the development. These forces can themselves moderate or shape the impact of the propelling/constraining forces as well as being moderated or shaped by them. This dynamic interplay between different settings and different types of forces affords the teacher wishing to develop a pedagogy for autonomy much room for manoeuvre; by analysing this interplay, *the teacher can be empowered to find effective ways of justifying and arguing for the development of pedagogy for autonomy, even in contexts which at first glance appear to constrain its development.*

Language teachers are faced with paradoxes, and none more so than those who wish to develop a pedagogy for autonomy. In the case of language policies for Europe, the Common European Framework of Reference for Languages has as an explicit aim the development of foreign language teaching methods which "strengthen independence of thought, judgement and action, combined with social skills and responsibility" (Council of Europe, 2001a: 4), and promotes lifelong language learning. It does so by integrating as a basic principle the notion of self-directed learning, which includes "raising the learner's awareness of his or her present state of knowledge; self-setting of feasible and worthwhile objectives; selection of materials; self-assessment" Council of Europe, 2001a: 6) and by recommending an action-oriented methodology. The learner-centred nature of language learning is evident in the following definition of language use and learning:

> Language use, embracing language learning, comprises the actions performed by persons who as individuals and as social agents develop a range of *competences*, both *general* and in particular *communicative language competences*. They draw on the competences at their disposal in various contexts under various *conditions* and under various *constraints* to engage in *language activities* involving *language processes* to produce and/or receive *texts* in relation to *themes* in specific *domains*, activating those *strategies* which seem most appropriate for carrying out the *tasks* to be accomplished. The monitoring of these actions by the participants leads to the reinforcement or modification of their competences. (Council of Europe, 2001a: 9)

This is later reinforced by the inclusion of 'ability to learn' (*savoir-apprendre*) as an explicit competence to be developed by language learners that integrates language and communication awareness, study skills and heuristic skills (ibid.: 106–108).

In some contexts the promotion of autonomy is supported by some of the conditions and forces described above. In other contexts, however, some of the above conditions and forces will act as constraints and teachers may develop a sense of frustration, disempowerment, and inability to move forward in ways to which they are committed. It is to be hoped, however, that by analysing the context in which they are operating, teachers will be able to find ways forward. Lamb (2000b) argues that it is vital that teachers reflect critically on their setting and the forces which come into play, in order to be able to identify and reappraise critically their own personal theories, to articulate ideals, and to find ways of moving ever closer to those ideals: "(...) rather than feeling disempowered, they need to empower themselves by finding the spaces and opportunities for manoeuvre. (...) Critique (resistance) needs to be linked to transformation rather than resignation" (ibid.: 127).

3.2 Putting the learner on the map

Learner autonomy is nowadays accepted as a crucial educational goal and there is a consensus regarding the need to help students become more independent in how they think, learn and behave. Furthermore, within a constructivist framework, learning itself is perceived as having an autonomous nature. From the constructivist perspective, therefore, learning involves self-regulation and the construction of conceptual structures through reflection. However, no consensus has been reached as regards the definition of autonomy and what it actually entails. Our proposal draws on a broad theoretical background so as to enhance a holistic understanding of this concept and how it translates into learner competences.

3.2.1 Learner autonomy: definition and assumptions

Autonomy is one of the most fundamental aims of democratic education. From this perspective, the ultimate goal of education is to develop self-directed individuals who develop the capacity to make their own decisions about what they think and do (Boud, 1988; Brookfield, 1985; Candy, 1991; Knowles, 1975). In fact, autonomy in learning has long been part of a broad range of educational philosophies and it is currently identified as crucial to the development of lifelong learning in 'the learning society'. Moreover, it is often considered as a defining feature of all sustained learning that attains long-term success. Autonomy is both a goal of education and an educational approach to secure that goal. It is a central value in the modern world, a *prima facie* value that has dominated western culture since ancient times. In fact, its origin is said to be in ancient Greek philosophy in the notion of self-mastery and Augustine's *Confessions*. Since then a moral self-reflective, autonomous soul has been prevalent in the conceptualization of the individual in our tradition. The notion of autonomy places emphasis on the individual's self-governing abilities, the freedom and independence of one's deliberate actions from external manipulation and the capacity to decide for oneself.

The term 'autonomy' has sparked considerable controversy and debate to the extent that educationalists and applied linguists have not reached a consensus on a common definition. The debate has run for several decades in the language education field since Holec (1979: 3) first defined learner autonomy as "la capacité de prendre en charge son propre apprentissage", that is, an autonomous learner has the capacity to manage his/her own learning process by making the necessary decisions regarding learning goals, contents, resources, strategies, and assessment. Books and paper collections have been published worldwide exploring and accounting for theoretical and practical developments of the autonomy field in language (teacher) education, even though pedagogy for autonomy remains a marginal approach in the school setting (among others, see Barfield & Alvarado, 2013; Barfield & Brown, 2007; Barfield & Nix, 2003; 2011, 2001; Benson & Voller, 1997; Bobb-Wolff & Vera Batista, 2006; Cotterall & Crabbe, 1999; Dam, 1995; Dickinson, 1987; Ellis & Sinclair, 1989; Eriksson, 1993; Holec & Huttunen, 1997; Jiménez Raya & Lamb, 2008a; Jiménez Raya, Lamb & Vieira, 2007; Jiménez Raya & Vieira, 2015; Karlsson, Kjisik & Nordlund, 2001; Lamb & Reinders, 2006, 2008; Little, 1991; Little, Ridley & Ushioda, 2002; Littlewood, 1996; Miller, 2007; Oxford, 1990; Murray, Gao & Lamb, 2011; Palfreyman & Smith, 2003; Pemberton et al., 1996; Rubin & Thomson, 1994; Schwienhorst, 2016; Sinclair et al., 2000; van Lier, 1996; Vieira, 1998, 2009; Wenden, 1991; Wenden & Rubin, 1987).

The relevant literature is riddled with diverse interpretations of the notion of autonomy but one of the most obvious problems is the wealth of related notions such as 'independence', 'self-regulation', 'self-management', 'self-direction', 'self-instruction', 'learner development', and 'learning to learn'. Despite the lack of consensus on the definition, according to Sinclair's review (2000), there appears to be consensus over some of its features:

- it is a construct of capacity for self-management through conscious reflection and informed decision making

- it requires both willingness and ability to assume responsibility for learning
- it involves both independence and interdependence
- it develops and varies across time and circumstances
- it can be acquired naturally and in formal educational settings
- it has a political as well as a psychological dimension
- it may take different forms in different cultures

The above aspects are, of course, not specific to language learning and need to be understood with reference to the notion of the autonomous *person*. Littlewood (1996: 428) regards the autonomous person as:

> (…) one who has an independent capacity to make and carry out the choices which govern his or her actions. This capacity depends on two main components: ability and willingness. Ability depends on possessing both knowledge about the alternatives from which choices have to be made and the necessary skills for carrying out whatever choices seem most appropriate. Willingness depends on having both the motivation and the confidence to take responsibility for the choices required.

In sum, the autonomous person is someone who, within the limits of possibility, determines his/her life, establishes his/her own goals by evaluating their options in order to select the most worthy ones and acts in a rational and effective way to realize them. According to Ryan & Deci (2006), *autonomy* literally means regulation by the self as opposed to *heteronomy*, meaning controlled regulation, or regulation that occurs without self-endorsement. Dworkin (1988) maintains that people are autonomous only to the extent that their first order motives are (or would be) endorsed at a higher order of reflection. Autonomy-oriented individuals regulate their behaviour by reflecting on possibilities and choices, while control-oriented individuals tend to regulate behaviour by focusing on external rewards and punishments. However, as Boud (1988: 19) points out, *autonomy is more than acting on one's own*. It also implies *being creatively responsive to one's environment*, which means that autonomy grows from interacting in and with the world, and not in isolation.

As we have already stated, defining learner autonomy in a formal education context is not an easy task because of the complexity and multifaceted nature of the concept. It entails important psychological, philosophical, political, social, moral, and ideological implications and dimensions. In fact, as indicated by Dworkin (1988: 9), there seems to be no single conception of autonomy but one concept and various different conceptions of autonomy. Dworkin (ibid.: 29) adds that autonomy is understood "as a second-order capacity of persons to reflect critically upon their first-order preferences, desires, wishes and so forth and the capacity to accept or attempt to change these in the light of higher-order preferences and values". For Dworkin, the exercise of such capacity helps individuals define their nature, give meaning and coherence to their lives, and assume responsibility for the kind of person they are.

Any definition tends to present problems but a definition is necessary to give some indication of the parameters involved in the concept. For this reason, our definition of learner autonomy is provided as an *exploratory, analytic tool* that should stimulate further thinking and debate about autonomy in foreign language education. In chapter 2 above we defined learner and teacher autonomy as *the competence to develop as a self-determined, socially responsible and critically aware participant in (and beyond) educational environments, within a vision of education as (inter)personal empowerment and social transformation.* In the following sections we analyse seven assumptions that underlie this definition, with a focus on the learner:

> Autonomy is regarded as a competence
> Autonomy is not an absolute concept
> Autonomy involves self-determination
> Autonomy involves social responsibility
> Autonomy involves critical awareness
> Autonomy denotes a proactive and interactive role
> Autonomy is possible and desirable in educational environments

Autonomy is regarded as a competence

The notion of competence in this context entails abilities, knowledge, positive attitudes and dispositions towards agency and self-control in learning behaviours that are usually part of learning a foreign language in school. According to Cheetham & Chivers (1996), the notion of competence includes a functional component, a behavioural personal component, a cognitive component, and an ethical one. In addition, competence denotes the capacity to act responsibly and responsibility implies the ability to appreciate the consequences of acting (or not acting). In this context, competence entails, to our understanding, the ability to use knowledge, understanding, thinking skills and self-regulatory skills to perform effectively in learning. The notion of competence is empowering and has positive connotations as it implies the willingness and ability to grow as a person and learner and it is performance-oriented. This notion is broader than the notion of 'ability' favoured in previous definitions.

Autonomy is not an absolute concept

Autonomy is not an all or nothing concept. Autonomy is for certain a matter of degree and it is best understood as a continuum in which different degrees of self-management and self-regulation can be exercised at different moments and in different aspects of learning. The verb 'develop' in the definition also emphasises the developmental nature of both disposition and ability. In school, autonomy can be acquired through practice and experience. It is not something that you either have or do not have. Different learners may have developed autonomy to varying degrees of self-realization. A pedagogy for autonomy can help those learners who find it more difficult to manage their learning.

Autonomy involves self-determination

To be self-determined entails endorsing one's actions at the highest level of reflection (Ryan & Deci, 2006). According to self-determination theory, people are active organisms with innate tendencies toward psychological growth and development, who strive to master challenges and to integrate their experiences into a coherent sense of self. This natural human tendency does not operate automatically but instead requires ongoing stimulation and encouragement from the social environment to function effectively. The language classroom can either support or thwart the natural tendencies toward active engagement and psychological growth. Classrooms that promote and support autonomy are creating the conditions for the development of intrinsic motivation, active engagement in learning, discourse power, initiative and decision-making, self-control, and persistence in foreign language learning.

Autonomy involves social responsibility

This trait points to the social dimension of autonomy. One of the myths of autonomy is that it takes place in isolation. In order to truly understand the impact of learner autonomy, both as a pedagogical option and as a personality characteristic, it is essential to be aware of the social milieu in which such activity transpires. Language education towards the goal of autonomy is inescapably linked to belonging. In turn, belonging is regarded as an individual's perception of him/herself as being involved or committed to a social group or groups (Aviram, 2000). Developing social responsibility involves becoming aware of group needs and interdependence relationships. An individual who develops a consciousness of the group begins to perceive the atmosphere in the group, to watch how people's interactions influence the productivity of the group, and to understand the impact his or her actions have on the group as a whole. Becoming socially responsible means using this consciousness to improve the group's ability to live and work together. Community building and developing a sense of social responsibility demand basic social skills such as communication, co-operation, negotiation, conflict management, and perspective taking.

Autonomy involves critical awareness

The rationalist conception of autonomy derived from Kant's view consists of reflection and rational decision-making. For Callan (1994: 35), the "self who owns and rules in the autonomous life" is located "in the reflective powers of the individual, as opposed to whatever might seem to fix identity prior to rational reflection". So in this model of autonomy, rational reflection and critical awareness have indeed priority over non-reflective commitments, and are understood as a unique basis of the self's actions and traits.

Although the notions of self-determination and social responsibility already entail some degree of critical awareness, we want to emphasise the idea that individuals and groups live in contexts of power and are subjected to ideological influences which can potentially disempower them or at least lead to pseudo, inauthentic forms of autonomy. In such a paradigm, autonomy requires the development of a critical awareness of these influences and an ability to resist them if appropriate (Lamb, 2000a/b). For example, does student self-assessment empower or discipline students (Tan, 2004)?

Autonomy denotes a proactive and interactive role

The noun 'participant' in our definition emphasises agency and self-regulation. To be an agent is to make certain things happen intentionally by one's actions. Agency embodies the endowments, belief systems, self-regulatory capabilities and distributed structures and functions through which personal influence is exercised, rather than residing as a discrete entity in a particular place (Bandura, 1997, 2001). The central features of agency enable people to actually play a part in their self-development, adaptation, and self-renewal with changing times. Knowles (1975) argues that there is convincing evidence that people who take the initiative in learning (proactive learners) learn more things, and learn better, than do people who sit at the feet of teachers passively waiting to be taught (reactive learners): "They enter into learning more purposefully and with greater motivation. They also tend to retain and make use of what they learn better and longer than do the reactive learners" (Knowles, 1975: 14). In addition, learner autonomy has a social side which involves the ability to interact with and learn from others, since learning takes place through interaction with other people. This emphasis is consistent with social interactionism, which stresses the dynamic nature of the interplay between teachers, learners and tasks and provides a conception of learning as occurring through interactions with other people (Feuerstein et al., 1979, 1980; Vygotsky, 1962, 1978).

Autonomy is possible and desirable in educational environments

The prominence of autonomy as an educational goal can be attributed mainly to developments in philosophy, political science, psychology of learning, pedagogy, and recent social changes. Modern society requires individuals who are capable of assuming responsibility for their own learning and development, organizing their own learning processes and developing knowledge and skills to respond to the evolving challenges of the knowledge society and to participate actively in it.

To a large extent, any environment (formal or informal, institutional or not) can be educational as long as one learns within or from it. However, we are particularly concerned about how learners can become active participants in schools, and specifically in classrooms. Learning in a classroom can best be referred to as a *structured game* (Aviram & Yonah, 2004) which is defined according to a certain set of rules and 'internal goals', so that those who play the game have to observe their constitutive rules, otherwise there would be no game. However, the rules of the game are not fixed and can be explored so as to open up spaces for flexible control. The notion of *flexible control* is applicable in educational environments where it is possible for the learner to move from states of no control to states of total control, and from states of full control to states of complete dependence. The control a learner exercises in his/her learning may range across maximal, moderate or limited degrees of control. It determines his/her degree of participation in the construction of educational environments and has implications for the development of autonomy as a lifelong learning competence.

In the following section we focus more specifically on competences for learner autonomy in language learning, which will give us a better idea of what we mean by the complexity and multifaceted nature of the autonomy concept.

3.2.2 Competences for learner autonomy in language learning

Is learner autonomy a matter of having a cognitive capacity, a question of certain dispositions and desires, or even the existence of some enabling force which encourages the learner to exercise autonomy? Is it several of these or something else entirely? Because there is no clear-cut answer to this question, we need to emphasise various competences that enable learner autonomy and which we group under the following headings:

Learning competence
Competence to self-motivate
Competence to think critically

Rather than assuming that pedagogy must integrate all the competences below, we want to highlight the multidimensionality of learner autonomy, as well as provide a conceptual tool that can help teachers *analyse* their own practice, *compare* it with alternative practices, and *expand* it in the direction they find most suitable to their students' learning needs and interests. For example, one may look at the list and ask: *What competences does my teaching favour, why and how? What competences might I help my students develop, why and how?*

Learning competence

Learning competence can be broadly defined as the competence to regulate and control mental activity through the application of metacognitive knowledge and the orchestrated use of learning strategies. Self-regulation theory captures well the major components of this competence. Zimmerman (1989: 329) defines self-regulated learners as *metacognitively, motivationally and behaviourally active participants in their own learning process*. A self-regulated learner typically sets personal goals, uses learning strategies, monitors progress, and adapts his/her approach to accomplish learning goals alone or in cooperation with others. This involves: a) metacognitive knowledge and beliefs about learning; b) learning strategies; c) attitudinal competence. Each of these aspects is explained below.

a) Metacognitive knowledge and beliefs about learning

Metacognitive knowledge refers to the part of one's acquired world knowledge that has to do with cognitive matters (the others being domain knowledge, i.e. that which is specific to the subject of linguistic theory, and social knowledge, concerning the social distance between themselves and the target culture and, as such, related to social psychological theories of motivation). This knowledge is similar in nature to other world knowledge that individuals have but focuses on general knowledge about cognitive activities and demands, as well as the features of one's own cognitive activities and capabilities. It can be used by the learner to control cognitive processes more effectively. In addition, it is said to be a stable body of knowledge, though it may change over time. Wenden (1999a/b) offers the following properties of metacognitive knowledge: it is a stable system of related ideas, although it may change with cognitive maturity and the ability to reflect on the learning process and to develop new assumptions; it is acquired unconsciously or consciously, but it can be brought to consciousness and talked about. Flavell (1979, 1987) divides metacognitive knowledge into three categories:

- *Person knowledge:* general knowledge about how human beings learn and process information, as well as individual knowledge of one's own intellectual strengths and weaknesses in language learning. It includes both cognitive and affective factors that facilitate learning.

- *Task* knowledge: knowledge about the nature and requirements of the different language learning tasks learners are asked to perform in lessons (e.g. listen and complete, read and summarise) as well as knowledge regarding the nature of language learning and its complexity. This category includes knowledge of the resources, steps and strategies involved in task completion and awareness of whether the task is easy or difficult.
- *Strategy* knowledge: knowledge about the role of strategies in the learning process, that is, knowledge about the most effective language learning strategies as well as knowledge about the best way to tackle language learning. It also includes principles for the choice of learning strategies.

The literature on metacognition also reminds us that metacognitive knowledge is not the same as metacognitive strategies, since the former is knowledge acquired about learning, whereas the latter are skills through which the learners manage, direct, regulate and guide their learning (Weinert & Kluwe, 1987; Wenden, 1999 a/b).

Learner beliefs are often used as a synonym for metacognitive knowledge (e.g. Victori, 1999). Drawing on Alexander & Dochy (1995), however, Wenden describes beliefs as being held 'more tenaciously' than metacognitive knowledge, and also differing in that they are 'value related' (Wenden, 1999 a/b). Lamb (2005b) distinguishes between metacognitive knowledge and beliefs as two types of knowledge; the first type is knowledge gained about the realities of learning in a particular context, and relates specifically to what learners know about themselves and their own learning contexts; the second is related to knowledge about learning in general, whose origins it is difficult to specify. He also explores the significance to motivation of levels of congruence and incongruence between metacognitive knowledge and beliefs. For example, beliefs about what makes a good learner are not always the same as knowledge about oneself as a learner.

b) Learning strategies

There has been considerable discussion of the idea that strategies are crucial in intelligent behaviour (Anderson, 1985; Baron, 1985a/b; Flavell, 1979; Sternberg, 1985, 1990). The claim has been that intelligence may consist to a large extent of a tendency to use certain strategies for learning, understanding, or problem solving. The importance of this claim, however, does not hinge on a notion of what strategies are the important ones; rather the significant point is that any limits on performance are not unmodifiable capacities. Furthermore, cognitive approaches to learning stress that learning is an active, constructive, and goal-oriented process that is dependent upon the mental activities of the learner. Probably the most important outcome of studies in this field has been the formulation of learning strategies in an information-processing theoretical framework. This model contains an executive function in addition to an operative one. A third category is concerned with the effects of social and affective purposes on learning. Within this framework, second language learning is viewed as the acquisition of a complex cognitive skill. According to McLaughlin, "To learn a second language is to learn a skill, because various aspects of the task must be practised and integrated into fluent performance" (1987: 133). This further requires the automatization of component sub-skills. In an information processing framework, learning strategies can be broadly defined as "steps taken by students to enhance their own learning" (Oxford, 1990: 1). They refer to specific actions or techniques that can be observable or invisible, conscious or unconscious, with a direct or indirect influence upon learning. Typologies of learning strategies have been proposed in the literature (see, for example, Ellis & Sinclair, 1989; O'Malley & Chamot, 1990; Oxford, 1990; Wenden, 1991; Wenden & Rubin, 1987), focusing mostly on three groups of strategies briefly described below: cognitive, metacognitive, and socio-affective strategies. It is usually assumed that metacognitive strategies are the ones that better contribute to self-regulated learning.

- *Cognitive strategies.* Cognitive strategies are used for manipulating mentally or physically information to be learnt in ways that enhance learning. These strategies contribute to deep processing of learning material and to the establishment of meaningful mental linkages. In this category we find strategies such as elaboration, translation, inferencing, induction, deduction, grouping vocabulary items, creation of mental images to facilitate retention of information, and transfer.
- *Metacognitive/self-regulatory strategies.* These help students regulate their cognitive activity by engaging in active planning, checking, testing, monitoring, revising, selecting strategies, analysing the effectiveness of learning strategies, and thinking about their performance. Because

they are central to self-regulation, they play a crucial role in learner autonomy:

Awareness of own level of understanding of language learning. This relates to an individual's evaluation of the degree of understanding s/he has of the goals and the description of language learning.

Directed attention. Deciding in advance to attend in general to a learning task and ignore irrelevant distractors; maintaining attention during the learning task.

Selective attention. Focusing attention on certain specific aspects of input and ignoring irrelevant ones.

Activating prior knowledge. This relates to the ability to bring to mind previous knowledge related to the present situation. In the context of language learning, it includes the ability to recall previously encountered language learning problems with similar features.

Regulation of strategies. This relates to one's ability to think about and use strategies that were effective in the past for similar situations and consciously apply those strategies. Executive regulation refers to decisions about the organization, effort, amount, course, and direction of one's own cognitive activity.

Regulation of actions/self-management. This refers to the ability to establish, develop, follow and update a plan of actions conducive to language learning. The plan comprises previewing the organizing principle of an individual learning task or a series of learning tasks, goal setting, definition of steps to be taken towards the goals, time setting, and selection of strategies and resources to be used. It relates to one's ability to foresee the actions that can lead to the successful accomplishment of the task of language learning. It also entails understanding the conditions that help one learn and making arrangements for the occurrence of those conditions.

Monitoring and evaluating one's learning process. Self-evaluation is a key aspect of the development of self-determination and social responsibility. Whenever possible, students should be involved in monitoring and evaluating their own development, individually and with others.

Evaluation of the steps taken in learning. This relates to one's ability to keep track of how well one is performing a learning activity. It is an evaluation of the actions taking into account the goals set.

Evaluation of the effectiveness of the strategy choice. This refers to individuals' judgement of their learning experience.

- *Socio-affective strategies.* These represent a broad category that involves either interaction with another person or control over emotion and affect; they are used for self-motivation and encouragement, to reduce anxiety, to promote interaction opportunities and co-operation with others. Strategies under this category include co-operation, self-talk, questioning for clarification, and self-reinforcement. It is relevant to highlight that learning is influenced by social interactions, interpersonal relations, and communication with others. Therefore, socio-affective strategies can have an indirect influence on leaners' ability to self-regulate learning.

Donato & McCormick (1994) have adopted a sociocultural perspective on learning strategies. Sociocultural theory maintains that emergence of strategies is a process directly connected to the practices of cultural groups through which novices develop into competent members of these communities. From this perspective, language learning tasks and contexts are regarded as situated activities that are continually under development and that are influential upon individuals' strategic orientations to classroom learning. Language learning strategies in this model are "actions motivated by specific objectives and are instrumental to fulfilling specific goals" (Donato & McCormick, 1994: 455).

It is important to note that metacognitive learning strategies promote 'learning to learn', therefore strategy development should be directly related to the nature of language learning tasks, which can be language-specific (e.g. reading strategies) or more cross-disciplinary (e.g. strategies to cooperate with others). This implies that the above strategy types may need to be broken down into more specific strategies. For example, the self-management of reading tasks involves specific strategies that are different from those involved in the self-management of writing tasks, and the identification of strategies in both cases derives from an understanding of what reading and writing entail. From this perspective, encouraging the use of metacognitive strategies along with the development of metacognitive knowledge will help learners understand what language learning is about and how they can best develop their competences as language users and learners.

c) Attitudinal competence

Attitudinal competence refers to the ability to generate positive attitudes towards the assumption of responsibilities in learning. Attitudes are intensive beliefs that predispose one to act and feel in certain ways. The notion of attitude is a psychological construct comprised of cognitive, affective, and intentional components that exert a decisive influence on motivation. Beliefs and attitudes related to language, language learning, and language teaching play a powerful role in affective responses to language learning. They are relatively stable, and they are the consequence of positive or negative experiences over time in learning a foreign language. Research on the good language learner and on the role of attitudes in language acquisition has identified the following attitudes as particularly relevant in the promotion of autonomy:

- active attitude towards learning
- seeking out learning opportunities
- willingness to show initiative in language learning activities, tasks, and language use
- willingness to take on responsibility
- willingness to take risks
- openness to cooperation
- intellectual curiosity
- tolerance of ambiguity
- confidence in one's ability to learn

Competence to self-motivate

Much has been said about the role of motivation in learning. According to Deci & Flaste (1995: 9), "self-motivation (...) is at the heart of creativity, responsibility, healthy behavior, and lasting change". Corder (1981) argued that, if motivation to do so were present, it was inevitable that a human being would learn a language. When we refer to a student's motivation to learn, our focus is on the student's desire to participate and be successful in the learning process. Motivation is an internal state or condition (sometimes described as a need, desire, or want) that serves to activate or energize student behaviour and give it direction (Kleinginna & Kleinginna, 1981). Motivation also addresses the reasons behind student interest or lack of interest in learning. While a number of students may appear to be equally motivated or unmotivated, the factors explaining their involvement in learning may be quite different. Maslow (1954) stated that human life would never be understood unless its highest aspirations were taken into account. From his perspective, growth, self-actualization, the quest for identity and autonomy, and the yearning for excellence must be accepted beyond question as a prevalent and perhaps universal human tendency. And yet there are also other regressive, fearful, self-diminishing tendencies as well.

Various authors have established a direct link between learner autonomy and motivation (see Deci & Ryan, 1985; Lamb, 2005b, 2009, 2011; Ushioda, 1996). Spratt, Humphries & Chan (2002) maintain that when motivation and autonomy are considered together, autonomy tends to be regarded as facilitating motivation, rather than the other way round, with motivation in turn leading to successful language learning. However, in their study, they concluded that motivation also facilitated autonomy and might indeed be a pre-condition for it. This finding can be applied both negatively, in that the absence of motivation seemed to inhibit the practice of learner autonomy, and positively, in that the interviews pointed to a strong relationship between higher levels of motivation and greater engagement in extra-class activity. For them this is a possible indicator of increasing autonomy.

According to Ames (1986), in order to measure learner effectiveness we need to take into consideration the learner's *beliefs, perceptions, interpretations, and expectations that enable him/her to become involved, independent, and confident in his/her own learning.* Even though the internal and external sources of motivation are complex and thus difficult to capture, there seem to be some factors of particular relevance for learner autonomy in a school context: *attributions, motivational beliefs, intrinsic motivation, and motivational self-regulation, or self-motivation.*

- *Attributions.* Attribution theory is the theory of how people explain the causes of their own and other people's behaviour. People typically make either external or internal attributions. External attributions assign causality to an outside agent or force. By contrast, internal attributions assign causality to factors within the person. In addition, these attributions are either under control or not under control. To understand the goals of learning and to be able to set them implies that we are relating to the goals. If we believe that we are initiating our activity and then controlling it, we are relating to that activity. Understanding what we are doing, and why and how we are doing it means that we are relating. Weiner (1992) identified ability, effort, task difficulty, and luck as the most important achievement attributions. They classified these attributions into three causal dimensions: locus of control, stability, and controllability. The locus of control dimension encompasses two poles: internal versus external locus of control. The stability dimension explains whether causes change over time or not. For example, ability was classified as a stable, internal cause, and effort was classified as unstable and internal. Controllability contrasts causes one can control, such as skill or efficacy, with causes one cannot really control, such as mood, aptitude, others' actions, and luck. Table 2 below shows the four attributions that can result from a combination of internal or external locus of control and whether or not control is actually possible.

Table 2. *Attribution types according to locus of control*

	External	Internal
Control	Task difficulty	Effort
No Control	Luck	Ability

- *Motivational beliefs.* There is evidence to suggest that "among the types of thought that affect action, none is more central than people's judgements of their capabilities to deal effectively with different realities" (Bandura, 1986: 21). Self-efficacy beliefs determine how people feel, think, motivate themselves and behave. Bandura defined self-efficacy as individuals' confidence in their ability to organize and execute a given course of action to solve a problem or accomplish a task; he characterized it as a multidimensional construct that varies in strength, generality, and level (or difficulty). Thus, some people have a strong sense of self-efficacy and others do not; some have efficacy beliefs that encompass many situations, whereas others have narrow efficacy beliefs; and some believe they are efficacious even on the most difficult tasks, whereas others believe they are efficacious only on easier tasks. These self-beliefs of efficacy play a key role in the self-regulation of motivation. High levels of motivation and performance have a reciprocal effect, thereby further enhancing self-efficacy beliefs. Conversely, low efficacy beliefs are characterized by low aspirations and weak commitments to goals. These individuals are more likely to become frustrated when they encounter difficult challenges, and see these challenges as personal threats to be avoided rather than challenges to be mastered (Bandura, 1993).

- *Intrinsic motivation.* As human beings, our need for autonomy comes from an inherent drive to retain a sense of agency over our own actions. Competence comes from our desire to be good at what we value. When individuals are intrinsically motivated, they engage in an activity because they are interested in and enjoy the activity. When extrinsically motivated, individuals engage in activities for instrumental or other reasons, such as receiving a reward. Given the growing evidence that extrinsic incentives and pressures can undermine motivation to perform even inherently interesting activities, Deci & Ryan (1985) proposed self-determination theory, contending that the primary psychological needs of autonomy, competence and relatedness lead individuals to seek and meet the challenges of life. The authors argued that people who access activities with the optimum level of challenge tend to find these activities intrinsically motivating because they fulfil a basic need for competence. In addition, they argued that intrinsic motivation is maintained only when learners feel competent and self-determined. When individuals are self-determined, their reasons for engaging actively in learning tasks are completely internalized (Grolnick et al., 2000). Deci and colleagues defined several levels in the process of going from external to internalized regulation. The theory places the various types of regulations on a continuum between self-determined (intrinsic) and controlled (extrinsic) forms of motivation, depending on how 'internalized' they are, that is, how much the regulation has been transferred from outside to inside the individual. Five categories along the continuum have been identified: *external regulation* (coming from outside the individual, such as rewards and threats); *introjected* (internal regulation based on feelings that one has to do the behaviour); *identified* (internal regulation based on the utility of that behaviour, e.g., studying hard to get grades to get into college); *integrated* (regulation based on what the individual thinks is important and essential to the self); and pure *intrinsic regulation.*

To be self-determined is to endorse one's actions at the highest level of reflection. When self-determined, people experience a sense of freedom to do what is interesting, personally important and vitalizing (Deci & Ryan, 1985). The application of the intrinsic/extrinsic continuum can be useful in organizing language learning goals systematically. According to Noels (2001), this paradigm is predominantly useful for analysing the classroom climate and the FL teacher in terms of how much they either control or promote autonomy, a dimension of contrast which has immediate practical implications for the development of learner autonomy and self-regulation in language teaching. In addition, self-determination theory suggests that motivated behaviours vary in the degree to which they are autonomous vs. controlled. Autonomous behaviours have an internal locus of causality, are experienced as volitional, and are performed out of interest or personal importance. Intrinsically motivated behaviours are the prototype of autonomy (Black & Deci, 2000). Learning that promotes intrinsic motivational processes is mostly learning that is full of personal meaning and relevance (Ushioda, 1996).

- *Motivational self-regulation*, or *self-motivation*. An exciting perspective within motivational psychology explores ways in which we can provide learners with the appropriate knowledge and skills to motivate themselves. Self-motivation implies taking charge of the affective dimension of the language learning experience and it requires positive (self-)beliefs as well as intrinsic motivation. It is basically a capacity for effective motivational thinking that fulfils an active functional role in promoting and sustaining learner autonomy (Ushioda, 1996). *Self-motivation* simply means to act with a sense of agency. While we strive to internalize, or attain a sense of control over the external pressures in our lives, we experience varying levels of success in doing so.

Competence to think critically

As Dearden (1972: 70) puts it, the development of personal autonomy as an educational goal "is the development of a kind of person whose thought and action in important areas of his life are to be explained by reference to his own choices, decisions, reflections, deliberations – in short, his own activity of mind". The autonomous person is one who makes his/her own choices and subjects them to rational assessment and criticism. As Benn (1976: 123) remarks, "To be a chooser is not enough for autonomy". Autonomous choice has to be rationally informed. Human beings are rational animals and in exercising their intellectual powers they realise their own essence, that is, their autonomy. Critical thinking is, therefore, according to Siegel (1988), co-extensive with rationality and autonomy.

Critical thinking is the intellectually disciplined process of actively and skilfully conceptualizing, applying, analysing, synthesizing, and/or evaluating information gathered from, or generated by, observation, experience, reflection, reasoning, or communication, as a guide to belief and action. Those who become critical thinkers acquire such intellectual resources as background knowledge, operational knowledge of appropriate standards, knowledge of key concepts and possession of effective heuristics, and of certain vital habits of mind. This implies the capacity to be moved by reasons and to appreciate and accept the relevance and evidential force of reasons for beliefs and actions (Bailin et al., 1999). This conception views competence in critical thinking in terms of intellectual resources.

The competence to think critically is coextensive with the notion of autonomy. Given the conceptual link between autonomy and rationality, the educational ideal of critical thinking becomes indistinguishable from that of rational autonomy (Cuypers, 2004). A critical thinker is one who has the ability to assess reasons in the light of epistemic and logical criteria (Siegel, 1988). However, having the intellectual resources necessary for critical thinking does not, by itself, make one a critical thinker. One must also have certain commitments, attitudes or habits of mind that dispose him or her to use these resources to fulfil relevant standards and principles of good thinking. Accordingly, thinking critically entails appreciating reasons and caring about their evidential power; it also entails a desire and willingness to evaluate reasons and the evidence objectively according to impartial and non-arbitrary standards.

Essentially, reflection is linked to elements that are fundamental to meaningful learning and cognitive development: the development of metacognition, the ability to self-evaluate and higher-level thinking skills (problem-solving, decision-making...), the ability to ensure that learning needs are met within a context of negotiation and compromise. In order to develop their learning capacity, learners need to develop sound criteria and standards for analysing and assessing their own thinking. Autonomous choice has to be authentic as well as rationally informed. As defined above critical thinking can be regarded as having two basic components: (a) a set of skills to process and generate information and beliefs, and (b) the habit, based on intellectual commitment, of using those skills to guide behaviour. This view entails that a critical thinker must not only be able to think critically, but must also be willing or otherwise disposed to doing so. What Siegel (1988) calls the 'critical spirit' involves certain dispositions, attitudes, and character traits. Critical thinkers must be able to reflect on the relevance and adequacy of the principles of thinking they are using at any particular moment. This is feasible only if their primary commitment is to responsible belief and action rather than to particular principles of good thinking. Within this general conception of critical thinking, a critical thinker shows the following attributes:

- asks pertinent questions and is interested in finding new solutions
- assesses statements and arguments
- is able to admit a lack of understanding or information
- is willing to examine beliefs, assumptions, and opinions and weigh them against facts
- regards critical thinking as a lifelong process of (self-)assessment
- looks for evidence to support assumptions and beliefs
- suspends judgment until all facts have been gathered and considered
- is able to adjust opinions when new facts are found
- examines learning problems closely
- is critically aware of contexts, especially of variables that affect learning
- is able to negotiate and find positive strategies to make his/her voice heard

All the competences presented so far should be seen as interrelated rather than isolated components of learner autonomy. However, different practical approaches tend to emphasise them differently, and we might even say that it is impossible to think of a pedagogy that embraces all of them explicitly and intentionally. As we said before, it is not our intention to suggest that pedagogy for autonomy must foster them all. On the one hand, many of these are largely invisible and internally controlled, and not much is known about how they develop or how their development can be promoted. On the other hand, not all of them will be equally relevant for different learners or in different contexts. Moreover, we have to take into account the limitations of pedagogical action itself, and also the provisional nature of any pedagogical choices a teacher makes at a certain moment in his/her professional life. What we suggest is that teachers enquire systematically into teaching with the above competences in mind and thus develop their professional competence to the benefit of *learning*. Therefore, we now invite you to think about your *teaching approach* (strategies, materials, textbook…) and use Table 3 below to reflect about *whether it promotes competences for learner autonomy*:

> *Does my teaching promote/facilitate…?* [√ – Yes, X – No, ? – I can do better]
> *What aspects of… should I focus on more?* [identify them]

Table 3. *Reflection on promoting competences for learner autonomy*

COMPETENCES FOR LEARNER AUTONOMY

1. LEARNING COMPETENCE

Does my teaching promote/facilitate the development of learning competence? What aspects of learning competence should I focus on more?

Metacognitive knowledge and beliefs about learning
_____ person variables _____ task variables _____ strategy variables

- -

Learning strategies

Cognitive Strategies

_____ elaborate	_____ translate	_____ infer	_____ induct
_____ deduct	_____ group items	_____ create mental images	_____ transfer

Metacognitive/ self-regulatory strategies

_____ be aware of own level of understanding	_____ direct attention
_____ pay selective attention	_____ activate prior knowledge
_____ regulate strategies	_____ regulate actions
_____ monitor and evaluate the learning process	_____ evaluate strategy choice

Socio-affective strategies

_____ lower one's anxiety	_____ cooperate/ask for cooperation
_____ encourage oneself	_____ take one's 'emotional temperature'

- -

Attitudinal competence

_____ take initiatives	_____ seeking out learning opportunities
_____ take on responsibility	_____ take risks
_____ cooperate	_____ be intellectually curious
_____ tolerate ambiguity	_____ trust one's ability to learn

2. COMPETENCE TO SELF-MOTIVATE

Does my teaching promote/facilitate the development of the competence to self-motivate?
What aspects of motivation should I focus more on?

Attributions
_____ internal attributions (ability, effort...)

Motivational beliefs
_____ sense of self-efficacy   _____ sense of commitment   _____ high aspirations

Intrinsic and self- motivation
_____ sense of competence _____ sense of agency   _____ interest
_____ engagement   _____ self-determination   _____ intrinsic regulation

---

3. COMPETENCE TO THINK CRITICALLY

Does my teaching promote/facilitate the development of the competence to think critically?
What aspects of critical thinking should I focus more on?

_____ ask pertinent questions and find new solutions
_____ assess statements and arguments
_____ admit lack of understanding or information
_____ examine beliefs, assumptions, and opinions and weigh them against facts
_____ regard critical thinking as a lifelong process of (self-) assessment
_____ look for evidence to support assumptions and beliefs
_____ suspend judgement until all facts have been gathered and considered
_____ adjust opinions when new facts are found
_____ examine learning problems closely
_____ be critically aware of contexts, especially of variables that affect learning
_____ negotiate and find positive strategies to make one's voice heard

3.3 Putting the teacher on the map

This section focuses on how teacher autonomy is related to learner autonomy and how teaching can enable pedagogy for autonomy. It is our assumption that pedagogy for autonomy entails both learner and teacher empowerment. As with previous sections, these issues are not a prerogative of foreign language education and can be addressed via cross-disciplinary dialogue and action in schools.

3.3.1 Teacher autonomy towards learner autonomy

It is perhaps surprising, to say the least, that a lot of well-known publications on language learner autonomy undervalue or fail to integrate issues of teacher autonomy (just have a look at book titles, tables of contents and indexes). This is also true of major projects for establishing European frameworks of reference for language teaching, learning and assessment (Council of Europe, 2001a), and language teacher education (Kelly et al., 2004). As regards national policies and teacher development programmes, these often rest on a view of the teacher as someone who is expected to implement external knowledge and prescriptions, even when autonomy is advocated by their proponents. To a large extent, we still need to acknowledge more clearly the *ideological nature of teaching* rather than adopting a neutral stance as regards its social role, especially since pedagogy is not a value free practice. Freire's well-known book *Pedagogia da Autonomia. Saberes Necessários à Prática Educativa* (Pedagogy of Autonomy – Necessary Knowledges for Educational Practice), first published in 1996, offers a holistic understanding of what teaching for autonomy *demands* from teachers as transformative educators who understand that education is an ideological struggle against oppressive ideologies, and also a form of critical intervention in the world. From this perspective teacher empowerment is a condition for learner empowerment and educational change.

By dismissing or undervaluing the issue of teacher autonomy in promoting learner autonomy in schools, we may be encouraging:

- a culture of pedagogy for autonomy as technical expertise, detached from a view of teaching as a moral and political act;
- a culture of teacher education towards learner autonomy that builds on an image of teachers as consumers of academic knowledge, rather than creative producers of practical knowledge, decision-makers and agents of change;
- a culture of research into learner autonomy that undervalues teachers' knowledge and experience and the role of school-based, teacher-led enquiry in promoting pedagogical innovation.

A critical rational conception of autonomy further holds that the autonomous person makes his/her own choices and subjects them to rational assessment and criticism. Three essential dimensions can be identified in this conception of autonomy: (a) choice, (b) authenticity, and (c) rational reflection. Studies in several domains have found the effects of autonomy supportive vs. controlling social contexts on learning and well-being outcomes to be mediated by participants' autonomous motivation while engaging in the behaviour (e.g. Williams et al., 1996); if teacher autonomy is undermined, teacher motivation will be affected negatively. There is increasing evidence that when people are coerced, they react with resistance, loss of energy and even resentment – the opposite of motivation. On the contrary, professionals whose initiatives are self-motivated tend to be high-performing and more persistent in their efforts.

What then, do we mean by teacher autonomy and how does it relate to learner autonomy? Let us start by recalling our definition of teacher autonomy: *the competence to develop as a self-determined, socially responsible and critically aware participant in educational environments, within a vision of education as (inter)personal empowerment and social transformation.* We take this definition as a *working hypothesis*, and the next section tries to operationalize it with a focus on teaching towards the development of teacher and learner autonomy. Before that, we need to focus on the particular vision of education it assumes and clarify what is involved in teacher autonomy as we see it.

By defining learner autonomy and teacher autonomy in the same way, we want to stress their interconnectedness. Nevertheless, this is not a straightforward issue. There seems to be agreement among some researchers of language learner autonomy that its development depends on teacher autonomy, although this idea has been expressed in slightly different ways, as in the examples below:

> Teacher autonomy can be defined as the teacher's ability and willingness to help learners take responsibility for their own learning. An autonomous teacher is thus a teacher who reflects on her teacher role and who can change it, who can help her learners become autonomous, and who is independent enough to *let* her learners become independent. (Thavenius, 1999: 160)

> In order to allow learners the opportunity to develop autonomy, teachers must themselves exercise autonomy in relation to their practice. (Benson, 2000: 117)

> (…) the development of learner autonomy depends on the development of teacher autonomy. By this I mean two things: (i) that it is unreasonable to expect teachers

to foster the growth of autonomy in their learners if they themselves do not know what it is to be an autonomous learner; and (ii) that in determining the initiatives they take in the classrooms, teachers must be able to exploit their professional skills autonomously, applying to their teaching those same reflective and self-managing processes that they apply to their learning. (Little, 2000: 45)

Doubts have been raised, however, as to whether teacher autonomy *necessarily* entails a concern for learner autonomy. In fact, the concept of teacher autonomy is highly complex and has been defined variously (see Contreras, 2002; Jiménez Raya, 2007, 2014). If we reduce its meaning to 'individual freedom from external control and self-directed teaching' (i.e. being free and able to teach as you like), then teacher autonomy may serve different purposes, including the reproduction of the *status quo*. However, if we situate it in a broader social and political perspective, which is what we seek to do, there is a sense that teacher and learner autonomy become interconnected.

In order to clarify this interconnectedness, a crucial question needs to be asked: "Do we view autonomy as the 'authoring of *one's own world*', or do we view it as the 'authoring of *our collective world*'?" (Benson, 2000: 117). Our answer depends largely on our vision of education. If we value *(inter)personal empowerment and social transformation* as educational goals, then autonomy becomes *a collective interest* and a *democratic ideal*, so that teacher and learner autonomy are like two sides of the same coin. In other words, teacher autonomy will be in the service of learner autonomy only to the extent that a philosophy of education based on democratic values is embraced. Furthermore, if we accept that autonomy is a central value to be promoted through education, then it must be central for any individual, including for the teacher who is expected to act as an autonomous professional.

Assuming that "the pursuit of learner autonomy and the pursuit of democracy in education are one and the same" (Little, 2004: 124), and taking into account that the pursuit of democracy in education (as in society at large) is fraught with dilemmas and constraints in most settings, then we can understand why it is necessary to envisage pedagogy for autonomy as *a cultural and political project* where resistance, critique and subversion become crucial components of teachers' professional competence (see Benson, 1997, on the de-politicization of autonomy). From this perspective, teacher autonomy entails critical awareness of the historical and structural conditions and forces pointed out in section 3.1 above. It further involves enquiring into the justifications for and implications of one's pedagogical choices:

> What do my practices say about my assumptions, values, and beliefs about teaching? Where did these ideas come from? What social practices are expressed in these ideas? What is it that causes me to maintain my theories? What views of power do they embody? Whose interests seem to be served by my practices? What is it that acts to constrain my views of what is possible in teaching? (Smyth, 1989: 7)

Through problematizing educational situations as social constructions amenable to change, teachers can gain new understandings of their personal theories and practices, challenge constraints and envisage alternative ways to teach, thus becoming more fully aware of the ideological nature of teaching:

> (...) the emphasis is upon forces making teaching the way it is, and how these forces act to reproduce, sustain, and maintain what often amount to the alienating status quo. (...) The difference is one of teaching being construed as an intellectual process (or an intellectual struggle) in which the elements are argument, debate and contestation of ideas and practices, compared with the implementation of a set of technical or mechanical procedures to be dutifully administered by teachers. (Smyth, 1997: 1102–1103)

The idea that reflective practitioners can use reflection as a tool for social criticism and reconstruction is contrary to an idyllic view of teachers working in peaceful learning communities. On the contrary, it implies individual and collective commitment to working in contexts where antagonistic ideas and conflicting interests and values emerge, constraints and dilemmas have to be faced, and everlasting tensions (authority vs. freedom, conservatism vs. change...) have to be managed. Therefore, developing professional autonomy (and pedagogy for autonomy) is essentially about *shortening the distance between reality and ideals, through opening up possibilities for education in schools to become more rational, just and satisfactory.*

On the basis of what has been said so far, teacher autonomy (like learner autonomy) can be seen as a relational competence where self-determination is both constrained and enhanced by social responsibility, which means that its growth rests on the interdependence between Self and Other. It evolves through direct or mediated dialogue with significant voices in the educational community, negotiation and compromise, moral sensitivity to problem situations, openness to diversity and critical awareness of contexts, participation in decision-making and voice. All this is in the service of (inter)personal empowerment and social transformation.

3.3.2 Enabling pedagogy for autonomy

Smyth (1987: 6) points out that "the notion that there are some groups who are equipped through intelligence and training to articulate what another group *should do and think*, is an anti-educational view". This is a reminder of what this section is intended to be: a springboard for critical reflection about enabling pedagogy for autonomy, rather than a prescriptive set of rules. Practical approaches represent *local pedagogies* and only teachers can decide whether the enabling conditions we propose are relevant or not, depending on their own visions of education and working circumstances. In a very real sense, there cannot be *one* "practical theory" of pedagogy for autonomy that embraces the diversity of discourses and practices we encounter in schools. But there can be tools for reflection, like Table 4 presented below, that enhance dialogue among educators, make diversity more explicit, and encourage the construction of common understandings. Our proposal is driven by both theory and experience of working with school teachers (see Jiménez Raya & Vieira, 2015; Lamb, 2010a/b, 2012; Vieira, 2014a, 2014b) and it can also be useful to teacher educators as "teachers of teachers", having in mind a pedagogy of teacher education that aims at promoting teachers' autonomy as learners, or "teacher-learner autonomy" (Smith, 2000; Smith & Erdogan, 2008).

Rather than assuming the need to fulfil all the conditions on the Table below, our aim is to portray the *complexity* involved in teaching towards autonomy, thus discouraging a simplistic view. Moreover, if we see pedagogy for autonomy as a never-ending process whereby resistance is linked to transformation rather than resignation (Lamb, 2000a: 127), then

> (...) the most appropriate way for each one of us to teach is exactly the way that we do teach – provided only that we are committed to an ongoing investigation of just what it is that we do, with a view to enhancing the processes and outcomes both for our students and for ourselves. (Edge, 1999: 41)

This idea suggests that teachers' approaches to autonomy are deeply rooted in their professional history and will always be, in this sense, *autobiographical.*

The enabling conditions formulated as questions in Table 4 are grouped into four main dimensions of professional autonomy:

Developing a critical view of (language) education
Managing local constraints so as to open up spaces for manoeuvre
Centring teaching on learning
Interacting with others in the professional community

For each enabling condition, we invite you to ask yourself three questions:

Am I willing to...?   [self-reflection on personal values, beliefs, dispositions...]
Am I able to...?   [self-reflection on ability to enact values, beliefs, dispositions...]
Do I have the opportunity to...? [self-reflection on professional situations and self-agency]

You may also ask yourself *how relevant* these aspects are/might be for you and your students and *why*, and rephrase or expand them, cross them out or add new ones to the list.

Table 4. Reflection on conditions for enabling pedagogy for autonomy

A. DEVELOPING A CRITICAL VIEW OF (LANGUAGE) EDUCATION *Am I willing...am I able...do I have the opportunity to...*
<ul><li>understand myself and my students as agents of educational and social change?</li><li>see teaching as an enquiry-oriented activity (as situations are often unique, uncertain and problematic)?</li><li>keep informed about approaches to language education and how they can promote learner autonomy?</li><li>realise the role of language education in promoting plurilingual/cultural competence?</li><li>be open and encourage learners' openness to linguistic and cultural diversity?</li><li>take a critical stance towards values and ends of language education in school curricula?</li><li>take a critical stance towards the educational value of syllabi, textbooks or other instructional materials?</li><li>encourage learners to be critical towards social and educational values and practices?</li></ul>

B. MANAGING LOCAL CONSTRAINTS SO AS TO OPEN UP SPACES FOR MANOEUVRE
Am I willing...am I able...do I have the opportunity to...

- uncover constraints on autonomy (my own and the learners') and face dilemmas as integral to teaching?
- challenge school routines and conventions (be subversive if necessary)?
- compromise between tradition and innovation without losing my ideals?
- shape pedagogical choices so as to open up possibilities for greater learner autonomy?
- share my pedagogical beliefs and concerns with learners?
- involve learners in finding creative solutions to problems that affect their learning?
- accept disagreement and conflict as dimensions of classroom communication and decision-making?
- articulate the personal aspects of learning (individual expectations, needs and interests) with the social/interactive nature of the classroom/school culture?

C. CENTRING TEACHING ON LEARNING
Am I willing...am I able...do I have the opportunity to...

- foster the learners' self-esteem and willingness to assume responsibility for learning?
- involve learners in reflection about language and the language learning process?
- foster knowledge of and experimentation with language learning strategies (in and outside class)?
- foster the self/co-management of language learning activities (planning, monitoring and evaluation)?
- foster the negotiation of ideas and decisions with and among learners?
- encourage co-operation and team work among learners?
- find ways to enhance the formative role of [self-]evaluation and [self-]assessment (e.g. through self-evaluation and negotiation of assessment)?
- collect and analyse learner data so as to understand and improve teaching and learning (e.g. through observation, questionnaires, checklists, diaries, portfolios, interviews, etc.)?
- encourage learners to collect and/ or analyse learning data so as to understand their learning?

D. INTERACTING WITH OTHERS IN THE PROFESSIONAL COMMUNITY
Am I willing...am I able...do I have the opportunity to...
• share my theories, practices and concerns with significant members in the professional community?
• invite others (learners, peers, mentors, etc.) to help me improve teaching and learning (e.g. through observation and feedback, material production, analysis of students' work, etc.)?
• disseminate experiences and confront my voice with other voices in the professional community?
• participate in public debate on issues regarding schooling and education in general?

In going through the Table (as teachers or teacher educators), we may find that:

- for each item, though "willingness", "ability" and "opportunity" may be interconnected, the presence of one does not guarantee the presence of the others;
- lack of "opportunity" becomes more evident when teacher choice is limited, or in school cultures that favour conservatism, individualism and isolation; it depends largely on external constraints, but also on how we view our role in relation to constraints (self-agency);
- different approaches may emphasise the various conditions differently, and some approaches may be more far-reaching than others in terms of promoting teacher/learner autonomy;
- trying to find reasons for our responses and reflecting on why some conditions are/might be relevant for us and our students leads to the kind of self-questioning suggested by Smyth (1989, see section above);
- "yes/no" answers will often turn into "maybe/ possibly" answers as we start to envisage possibilities that move our mind from what we usually think and do towards what we *can* think and do;
- the questions may help us identify personal strengths and needs, and thus establish priorities in terms of future (self-)development.

As we suggested before, developing autonomy is about shortening the distance between reality (what *is*) and our ideal (what *should be*), by extending the limits of freedom and exploring new territories (what *can be*). In practical terms, this often means taking small steps, as in the examples presented in Table 5. These and other examples can be analysed in terms of which conditions from the table above are being explored, especially as regards the possibilities envisaged.

Table 5. Examples of the exploration of the space of possibility in language teaching

My ideal (what should be)	Reality: action & constraints (what is)	Possibilities (what can be)
e.g. I wish I could give my students more opportunities for decision-making as regards learning activities	e.g. I don't give students much choice as I must cover the syllabus and follow the prescribed textbook so that they can pass the tests	e.g. Before tests, ask students to identify their own difficulties and let them choose what to do according to their needs; I could also negotiate or let them choose homework activities
e.g. I wish my students were more motivated to correct their own written mistakes as a way to develop self-regulation strategies and develop a positive attitude towards error	e.g. I often signal mistakes and use a code for self-correction, but some students, especially those with more language problems, find it boring, difficult, tiring, or time-consuming; I always need to bring extra activities to keep the faster ones busy, which creates different learning opportunities in class	e.g. I could select sets of mistakes from written assignments for group correction; groups might present their work to the class so as to encourage collaboration and give everyone the opportunity to reflect about a larger set of mistakes As students get used to this practice, they could themselves select mistakes for self/peer-correction
e.g. I wish my students were more motivated to read literary texts as part of their personal growth and cultural competence	e.g. I do my best to involve them in reading tasks. Unfortunately, the literary texts prescribed in the syllabus are often detached from their lives and they find them quite boring.	e.g. we could centre our analysis of literary texts on what makes them interesting/ boring for readers, reflect on students' own experience as readers, discuss the value of literature in our syllabus and contrast the prescribed texts with student-selected home readings
e.g. I wish I could have someone (a critical friend) to visit my classes and help me analyse and improve my teaching, as well as have the opportunity to see others teaching	e.g. I never felt at ease to ask one of my colleagues to engage in peer-coaching; I fear they may not be willing to, and I also fear my own reaction to an outside observer – am I ready for this kind of self-exposure?	e.g. I could ask one of my colleagues to look at my lesson plans and materials and give me some feedback; I could also offer to do that for him/her; if things turn out interesting for both, we could start collaborating more and maybe later we could engage in peer-coaching

Even when changes look too small, they can make a difference in the quality of teaching and learning. And even when nothing seems to be amenable to change, there is always something to be explored. In order to illustrate these ideas, imagine the following situations and their pedagogical implications (Vieira, 2010):

Imagine that every lesson you let your students chat in the FL for 5 minutes, in pairs or small groups, about any topic they like. How will this improve their talking time in class, their interactive skills, their motivation to use the FL, and their sense of belonging to a community that values their experience, interests and points of view?

Imagine that every two weeks you give your students 10 minutes to note down questions and doubts, collect them, and provide feedback or remedial work in the weeks that follow. How will this increase their awareness of learning and ability to identify and solve problems, as well as your own knowledge of learning and your ability to adjust teaching to your students' needs?

Imagine that whenever you ask the class a difficult question (on a grammar topic, a text they've read or a topic you are discussing) you give the students 1 minute to think about it and share ideas with a partner before they reply. How will this increase participation levels, reflective and cooperative skills, the chance that they come up with an interesting answer, and also their sense of accomplishment?

Imagine that whenever you introduce a new kind of activity in class you ask the students to reflect about its usefulness after completing it. How will this increase their awareness of task relevance and the chance that they better understand why they are learning the way they do, and how that improves their learning abilities?

Of course, teachers may be willing and have the opportunity to develop more structured experiences. A simple example is presented below, inspired by a more elaborate action research project carried out by a group of English teachers in a teacher education setting (presented in Vieira, 2014a). The focus is on making homework activities more learner-centred.

A Pedagogical Experience About HOMEWORK!

What is the real usefulness of doing homework? How do students feel about homework? What competences can homework promote in the students? Are students aware of the role of homework in their learning?

These were some of the questions that led a group of teachers of English to reflect about homework and involve their students in that reflection. As teachers, they certainly valued homework, but they also felt that many students didn't. Why was that? In order to find out about their students' attitudes towards homework, they asked them to fill in a self-reflection questionnaire. One of the questions was:

What ideas do you associate with <u>homework</u> in our classes? [√: A lot ?: Not much X: Not at all]

Pleasure	
Interest	
Freedom	
Creativity	
Challenge	
Usefulness	
Learning	

By analysing the students' answers, the teachers found out that many students did not associate these ideas with homework. They discussed the results in class and the students said that homework was more like an "obligation", something the teacher told them to do. Most of the times it was "boring". Although they agreed that it is was important for learning, they did not really know why. They just said: "If the teacher asks us to do it, then it must be important for learning…". The teachers realised they really had to do something to change their students' attitudes towards homework!

Two strategies were then implemented by them:

1. Designing and proposing individual and cooperative homework tasks that were more learner-centred than usual. For example: doing research on a topic and presenting the topic in class; choosing a favourite movie or book and telling the class about it; interviewing someone and telling the class about the person they interviewed; writing a poem or a story and reading it in class…

2. Making the students more aware of the different roles that homework can play in their learning, and involving them in monitoring homework by using the following checklist regularly (once a week):

	Homework dates				
A. My homework helped me to… [√:Yes / X:No]					
1. Revise what I learnt in class					
2. Expand what I learnt in class					
3. Develop study habits and learning strategies					
4. Develop my imagination and creativity					
5. Make choices according to my needs or interests					
6. Identify and surpass difficulties					
7. Be more active in class (e.g. contribute ideas)					
B. As I was doing my homework, I felt… [√:Yes / X:No]					
1. Motivated					
2. Self-confident					
3. Challenged to learn					

From time to time, the teachers asked each student to look at their checklist and discuss it with other classmates: *Were their opinions about their homework similar or different? Were they happy about their homework? Did they have any suggestion for the teacher?...* These aspects were discussed in pairs or small groups, and then with the teacher. The students' self-regulation checklists were collected every month for analysing data. The teachers observed that the students were now more interested in doing homework, more aware of its usefulness, and also more able to self-regulate learning. They decided to share their experience with other teachers in their schools and presented it in a professional conference.

In this example, it is possible to see that teachers develop a critical view of teaching by questioning a classroom routine – homework assignments – and making it more autonomy-oriented by questioning students about perceptions of homework, discussing those perceptions with them, exploring alternative practices that are more self-directed, and involving them in the self/co-regulation of learning. Table 6 presents the conditions regarding "Centring Teaching on Learning" as indicated in Table 5 above and can be used by teachers to analyse and design autonomy-oriented experiences. We can see that aspects of the homework experience above are integrated at least to some extent.

Table 6. Enabling conditions for centring teaching on learning (example)

A Pedagogical Experience About HOMEWORK!	
CENTRING TEACHING ON LEARNING *Does the pedagogical approach...*	
1. foster the learners' self-esteem and willingness to assume responsibility for learning?	√
2. involve learners in reflection about language and the language learning process?	√
3. foster knowledge of and experimentation with language learning strategies?	√
4. foster the self/co-management of language learning activities?	√
5. foster the negotiation of ideas and decisions with and among learners?	√
6. encourage co-operation and team work among learners?	√
7. find ways to enhance the formative role of [self-]evaluation and [self-]assessment?	√
8. collect and analyse learner data so as to understand and improve teaching and learning?	√
9. encourage learners to collect and/or analyse learning data so as to understand their learning?	√

Teachers often carry out innovative interventions aimed at promoting learner autonomy, even though those interventions are mostly occasional and developed in isolation. Educational innovation is a complex enterprise, depending on many factors. Ellis (2003: 322) points out the following attributes of innovation: teacher dissatisfaction with current practice, feasibility regarding working conditions, compatibility with teachers' existing styles and ideologies, relevance for the students' needs, complexity of the innovation itself, explicitness of its rationale, possibility of introduction step-by-step, observability of results by others, originality involved in implementation, and ownership, that is, the extent to which teachers feel they 'possess' the innovation. As we said before, pedagogy for autonomy remains a rather marginal approach in the school setting, where language education cultures are often too teacher-centred and content-driven. Under these circumstances, teachers' innovations towards autonomy will be complementary to mainstream approaches.

Given the constraints encountered in educational settings, one of the most important feelings within the process of change is *hope*: "to hope is to believe in possibilities" (Van Manen, 1990: 123). Pedagogical hope and professional autonomy go hand in hand in our struggle for a better education: education that is empowering for teachers and learners and that ultimately contributes to the transformation of society at large. If this sounds like a utopia, then it sounds right. Only *ideals* can push *reality* forwards, and not being able to fully accomplish them is just one more reason to keep on trying. From this perspective, dealing with complexity and uncertainty is integral to 're[ide]alistic' professional lifelong learning and 're[ide]alistic' pedagogies.

4. Principles for the development of pedagogy for autonomy

Our major goal throughout this book has been to establish a flexible framework for the development of learner and teacher autonomy at a school level. We now present a set of general principles that seek to operationalise that framework by integrating and elaborating on aspects from the previous chapters, with a global focus on *learning-centredness*.

4.1 The need for a principled methodological framework

The implementation of learning-centred approaches in the classroom has led to a number of different interpretations with regard to their implications for teaching. They have been characterized either by the use of information from learners in planning, implementing, monitoring and evaluating language programmes, or by student involvement in the decision-making process or in the implementation phase itself (Nunan, 1988). At the same time, learning-centredness has also been interpreted as a trend aiming to improve the language learner's ability to learn a language (Wenden, 2002). In general, learning-centred approaches focus on learners and on the learning process, which has important implications for the teacher's role as a facilitator and monitor of pedagogical processes. To justify learner involvement some researchers draw on constructivism, pointing out that knowledge may only be partly transmissible, and that learners normally reinterpret the information received through their own mental schemata anyway. Learner involvement, however, also rests on a view of pedagogy based on democratic values. By exercising democracy in the classroom, learners will become better prepared for democratic citizenship.

More than two decades ago, Thomas & Legutke maintained that there was:

> (...) a striking lack of learner autonomy or self-direction. Democratic principles appear alien to L2 classrooms. Learners do not participate in the management of their learning and teaching as actively and comprehensively as they could. Most of the responsibility for decision-making, content and process determination rests

> with the teacher alone. This is not only incompatible with recent claims of learner-centred methodologies, but also constitutes a major discrepancy with the overall educational goals of democratic societies. (Thomas & Legutke, 1991: 9)

Is this statement still true of modern language classrooms nowadays? And is it a problem that affects just modern language learning or schooling in general? From our perspective, there is still a huge mismatch between autonomy discourses and classroom practices. Several reasons for this can be pointed out: teacher-centred and content-driven traditions in (language) education are difficult to challenge, particularly when educational policies prioritise learning results over learning processes; the tensions between responsibility and freedom from constraint and control in educational systems often affect the extent to which learner autonomy can be developed; it has been difficult to reach a consensus on a practical notion of autonomy, its role in the modern language classroom and ways of promoting it; teacher education policies and practices do not seem to cover autonomy issues adequately.

Despite constraints, possibilities for innovation always exist, and the principles presented below are intended to provide a general methodological framework that allows for teacher and learner agency and responsible self-determination. Pedagogy for autonomy aims at creating and fostering in classrooms the conditions that support learners in becoming truly self-determined learners who can actively generate thoughts, feelings and actions which are systematically oriented towards the attainment of their language learning goals individually or in cooperation with others. Accordingly, pedagogy for autonomy must stimulate learners to become aware of the aims and processes of learning, foster critical reflection and help them develop skills, attitudes and beliefs that support self-regulation of the learning process. An autonomy supportive pedagogy also stimulates the development of intrinsic motivation by encouraging learner initiative, nurturing competence, using non-controlling communication, and creating rich language environments for language acquisition and use.

In our pedagogical proposal, Doughty's & Long's (2003) distinction between methodological principles and pedagogic procedures is particularly relevant. They define principles as putatively universally desirable modern language teaching design features, motivated by theory and research findings in SLA, language didactics, educational psychology, and elsewhere, which show them to be either necessary for language learning or facilitative of it (Doughty & Long, 2003). On the other hand, pedagogic procedures include the potentially infinite range of local options for realizing the principles at the classroom level. Choice among pedagogic procedures is determined by such factors as (a) teacher philosophy and preference; (b) learner age, proficiency, literacy level, aptitude and cognitive style; (c) the type of target linguistic features for which the procedures are to be used; and (d) the nature of the learning environment. Selection among the great variety of numerous existing pedagogic procedures available should vary, although rationally and systematically. One of the developments in this area is the European Language Portfolio, whose major pedagogical functions are: to facilitate reflective learning, to promote the transparency of language learning objectives and assessment criteria, to encourage self-direction and self-assessment, and to foster plurilingual/pluricultural competence and tolerance towards diversity (Council of Europe, 2001b).

4.2 Pedagogy for autonomy principles

Taking the distinction between principles and procedures as a starting point, we propose ten pedagogical principles that can be seen as interrelated *conditions that favour pedagogy for learner and teacher autonomy*. The fact that there are redundancies and intersections among these principles accounts for their interconnectedness in pedagogy for autonomy, and their separate presentation is intended to highlight distinct yet complementary foci and concerns. We hope that they will provide the basis for argument and for reflection, especially as their weighting can vary so as to accommodate the particular characteristics of the context, the teachers, and the learners. These principles involve *creating opportunities for and enhancing*:

Responsibility, choice, and flexible control
Learning to learn and self-regulation
Integration and explicitness
Autonomy support
Engagement and intrinsic motivation
Learner differentiation
Action-orientedness
Conversational interaction
Reflective enquiry
Formative assessment, assessment for learning and assessment for autonomy

Responsibility, choice, and flexible control

In modern language classrooms teachers typically shoulder most of the responsibility for learning in the classroom. However, many of the central concerns involved in autonomous learning can be summed up in the basic principle that learners should *assume responsibility for their own education*, that is, they should have a say and co-construct lessons. Assuming responsibility, according to Peters (2001: 59), means self-determination and self-responsibility in educational tasks. Responsibility is also a fundamental human need, according to Freire (1974). In order to satisfy this need it is necessary that the individual should take decisions in different matters of his/her life. For Deci & Ryan (1987: 1025) autonomy refers to "action that is chosen; action for which one is responsible". The learners' ability to make *choices* is concomitant with taking responsibility for their own learning, that is, assuming *control* of what they learn and why, how, what for, when and where.

Learners exercise their autonomy when they make authentic choices. According to Katz & Assor (2006), choice can be engaging and intrinsically motivating when the options provided are aligned with the learners' demand for the three basic psychological needs of autonomy, competence and relatedness. Thus, choice would be motivating when the range of options provided are important to the learners' goals and interests (autonomy), are not beyond the competence of the learner (competence), and are compatible with the students' social and cultural background (relatedness). For this reason, we should avoid equating choice with autonomy. From a self-determination perspective (Deci & Ryan, 1985, 2000), choice is a motivating experience in and of itself. So, when providing choice we should make sure that it is an autonomy-enhancing choice, that is, a choice that is perceived by learners as authentic and is consistent with their interests and needs. Ullmann-Margalit & Morgenbesser (1977) made an illuminating distinction between 'picking' and 'choosing.' For these authors, 'picking' does not automatically allow for the expression of the individual's desires or preferences, while choosing involves the existence of alternatives and there must be a reason or principle for the choice. Accordingly, in order to support autonomy it is important to avoid meaningless choice and increase opportunities for academically significant and personally relevant choice. Classrooms that support autonomy create the conditions for personal choice while providing structures that support individual success in learning.

As regards the notion of self-control, it has three main features: (1) it recognizes the capacity of the learner to exercise different levels of control at different moments; (2) these levels do not indicate distinctive and closed phases, but are placed on a continuous temporal axis; (3) the learner may shift from a minimal level of control, or even from absence of control, to a maximal level of control, according to the circumstances (Aviram & Yonah, 2004: 3). The notion of *flexible control* acknowledges the capacity of the learner to exercise different levels of control, as determined by the circumstances at different moments of the learning process.

Closely related with the notions of responsibility, choice and flexible control is negotiation. Breen & Littlejohn (2000) identify three types of negotiation: personal, interactive and procedural. Personal negotiation refers to an intrapersonal, psychological process of meaning-making inherent to the learners' internal search for understanding, whereas interactive and procedural forms of negotiation involve interaction with others, in the first case for the negotiation of meanings and in the second case for the negotiation of decisions. Procedural negotiation activates both personal and interactive negotiation and is particularly relevant for promoting a shared understanding of pedagogical processes and for enhancing learner self-management of the learning process. Self-management involves learners in planning, monitoring and evaluating their learning (Lamb, 2006; Wenden, 1991) and necessitates opportunities for learners to take control over at least some of the following:

- identifying learning interests and needs
- establishing learning objectives
- determining learning content
- planning learning activities
- choosing/building learning materials
- choosing learning methods and strategies
- making time and space arrangements
- monitoring and assessing learning
- monitoring and assessing teaching
- evaluating the teaching and learning process

Encouraging responsibility, choice and flexible control fosters the creation of spaces that enhance learner agency, voice and empowerment in modern language classrooms. It also allows teachers to mediate the curriculum from a learning-centred perspective and better adjust teaching to learners' goals, needs and interests. It is a matter of sharing control over what is learnt, how and what for, by enacting a dialogical approach whereby learners and teachers become co-constructors of pedagogy.

Learning to learn and self-regulation

A major goal of education is to help students develop the intellectual tools and learning strategies needed to learn. This can be done by encouraging greater *learning awareness,* more *effective and purposeful learning* through the enhancement of their metacognitive knowledge and beliefs, the resolute, reflective use of learning strategies, and the self-regulation of motivation and other affective variables. Three basic reasons are usually put forward to support the explicit focus on learning how to learn:

- Learners are not always willing to accept the challenge of learner autonomy and will therefore need to be supported.
- It is possible to develop one's learning potential through an explicit focus on learning strategies.
- Learners often have very distorted notions of what language learning actually entails.

Learning how to learn fosters the students' capacity to reflect on and verbalize their own learning process through *meta-learning* activities in order to improve their learning effectiveness (Jiménez Raya, 2003; Jiménez Raya & Pérez Fernández, 2002). The goal is to give learners the chance to gather their thoughts with regard to the language learning process, so that they can gain a new type of awareness that can result in higher degrees of motivation and efficiency. An explicit focus on learning how to learn helps learners develop the tools of learning and become more effective learners. It will also enable them to develop lifelong learning skills, which include the ability to deal with the unexpected, to make informed choices, to develop observational skills, to develop effective learning strategies, and to construct knowledge in one's interaction with the world.

The ultimate goal of learning how to learn is to enable learners to become better self-regulators. Self-regulation refers to the "self-directive process through which learners transform their mental abilities into academic skills" (Schunk & Zimmerman, 1998: 2). It refers to autonomous, academically effective forms of learning that involve metacognition, intrinsic motivation, and strategic behaviour. The metacognitive component includes planning, goal-setting, organizing, self-monitoring, and self-evaluating at various points during the process of learning. The motivational component emphasizes self-efficacy, self-attribution, and intrinsic motivation. Finally, the behavioural component refers to the selection, structuring, and creation of environments that enhance learning (Zimmerman, 2002). Self-regulation theory holds that learners can actively regulate their cognitive activity, motivation, or behaviour and, through these self-regulatory processes, achieve their goals and perform better. In order to manage their learning, learners need to learn how to exert control over both their learning environment and their own learning processes. Although self-regulation of learning can be promoted by teaching (Schunk & Zimmerman, 1998; Zimmerman & Risemberg, 1997), it is important to note that teachers should help learners amplify their repertoire of strategies and metacognitive knowledge and enhance their ability to make self-directed choices, rather than impose a unified model of learning or encourage the uncritical application of a predefined set of strategies.

In many situations, students are not given much choice in academic tasks or activities, they are not provided with explicit examples of strategic behaviours necessary to carry out complex learning tasks, and they are hardly ever given the opportunity to establish their own goals for their academic work, or to monitor and recognise their progress toward goals that are important to them. Language teachers must take a more active role in creating a learning environment which includes such self-management, whilst systematically cultivating learners' capacities to regulate their learning behaviours, emotions, cognitions, and environments. According to Zimmerman (1998:11), "optimal self-regulatory development appears to take root in socially supportive environments that provide extensive opportunities for self-directed practice."

To this end, teaching needs to help develop the necessary psychological functions that underlie self-regulatory processes (Shuell, 1988):

- Adequate choice of learning goals
- Adequate orientation to the learning goals
- Adequate planning of learning activities to match the goals set
- Awareness of goals and their relevance
- Intrinsic motivation for goals
- Ability to activate prior knowledge
- Volitional and emotional strategies (getting started, paying attention, self-esteem)

Summing up, in learning how to learn the learner should act at least partially as his/her own manager of change. The focus of change is his/her own self-concept and learning processes. This requires that the learner be able to conceptualize his/her own learning process and be able to pay attention to how s/he goes about learning. Learning how to learn can only be carried out productively in situations which do not threaten the learner. Learning to learn material needs to be personally relevant to the learner, and the learning experience and process have to be perceived as relevant to the learners' life experiences. The presentation of information about learning strategies and related areas is most effective when done through a variety of sensory modes and experiences, with sufficient repetitions and variations on themes, and when it is integrated carefully into the language learning tasks rather than being decontextualised. Finally, effective two-way communication with primary emphasis on learner talking and self-reflecting and teacher listening and reflecting is also another pedagogical feature of learning how to learn. Teachers' goals include not only facilitating language learning, but helping learners learn how to learn and self-regulate, developing effective learning strategies and greater awareness of the different aspects involved in language learning, as well as increased awareness of themselves as learners. The teacher is expected to guide learners in the exploration of their own way of learning and those of others.

By creating opportunities for learning how to learn and self-regulation, teachers will help their students become more aware of what language learning entails and more strategic and efficient as language learners. Moreover, teachers will better understand their students' attitudes, values and abilities, as well as their difficulties and the coping strategies they use. This will allow them to take an active role in reshaping students' learning approaches when needed.

Integration and explicitness

Pedagogy for autonomy involves the integration of communicative and learning competences, which means that learners *learn to use the language as they learn how to learn it*. Although learning to learn can be an isolated part of a programme, reports of practice in this area suggest that its impact is greatly enhanced if learners have the opportunity to appreciate its usefulness in communicative tasks and use regulation strategies in the context of task performance (Ellis & Sinclair, 1989; Wenden, 1991; Wenden & Rubin, 1987). For example, learners might be asked to use learning guides to support task performance (e.g., using a checklist of pre-/on-/post-writing strategies to conduct a writing task) or self-evaluate task performance as a basis for further improvement, with a focus on learning strategies and/or language outcomes. However, some learner training activities will focus on competences that are not language-specific (e.g. monitoring social skills in cooperative learning in groups), and others will focus on teaching rather than learning (e.g. evaluating a particular teaching strategy through a feedback questionnaire). Whatever the case, the idea is that learning to learn should be an integral part of the teaching approach, which entails making the rationale, aims and procedures of language and learner development transparent to the learners as a condition for learning awareness, involvement and participation (Sinclair, 1996). Pedagogical *explicitness* enhances a dialogic approach whereby teachers and learners become co-managers of the curriculum and critical agents of change.

Through integration and explicitness, learners are directly involved in reflection on what language learning is about and how it takes place. This relates directly to the development of metacognitive awareness and strategic ability, which means that the teacher becomes *a teacher of learning*.

Autonomy support

Research in the area of self-determination theory has found ample evidence regarding the relevance of *autonomy support* in developing intrinsic motivation in the classroom. Self-determination theory also recommends the examination of authority structures in teaching and their adaptation to support learner autonomy (Deci & Ryan, 1987; Ryan & Deci, 2000). This theory suggests that motivated behaviours vary in the degree to which they are autonomous or controlled. In language education contexts, autonomy support refers to what the teacher says and does in order to enhance learners' internal perceived locus of causality, volition and perceived choice during action (Reeve et al., 2004). Furthermore, it typically refers to the adoption of the learners' perspective by the teacher, acknowledging their feelings, and providing relevant information and opportunities for choice, while minimizing the use of pressures and demands (Black & Deci, 2000). According to research (Reeve, 2009; Reeve & Jang, 2006; Reeve et al., 2004), what teachers say and do to support autonomy can be characterized into three categories of instructional action: (a) foster inner motivational resources, (b) use non-controlling informational language, and (c) acknowledge the learners' perspective and feelings.

In addition, research has made a distinction between control-oriented and autonomy-oriented classrooms. Important benefits have been found in autonomy-oriented classrooms such as greater levels of engagement, higher quality learning, a preference for optimal challenge, enhanced intrinsic motivation, enhanced well-being and higher academic achievement (Guay, Ratelle & Chanal, 2008; Reeve et al., 2004; Vanteenkiste et al., 2004). If we accept the idea that autonomy requires the endorsement of one's own actions because they reflect one's personal goals, interests or values, then freedom of action in itself is not the most important feature. Freedom of action increases the likelihood that learners will be able to realize their personal goals and interests in their actions, however it is not the most important element in the need for autonomy. The most important element is the actual endorsement of one's actions where these actions are a reflection of one's personal goals, interests or values.

Three types of autonomy support have been identified: (a) organizational, (b) procedural, and (c) cognitive. Organizational autonomy support encourages student ownership of the environment and can include cooperation between the teacher and the students in choices over environmental procedures, such as developing rules in the classroom, or a certain degree of freedom when progressing toward a goal, such as setting due dates, for instance. A teacher encouraging organizational autonomy support would, for example, give his/her learners opportunities to:

- Choose group members
- Choose evaluation procedures
- Take responsibility for assignment deadlines
- Participate in creating and implementing classroom rules
- Choose seating arrangements

Procedural autonomy support "encourages student ownership of form" (Stefanou et al., 2004: 101), meaning that teachers take into account the students' own ways of working when developing a task as well as their freedom to present it. Typical areas learners are allowed to decide upon are:

- Choice of materials to use in class projects
- The ways in which competence will be demonstrated
- How to display work in an individual manner
- What they want or need to do
- How to handle materials

Finally, cognitive autonomy support encourages scaffolding and independent learning, promoting learners' evaluation of their own work, creating opportunities for them to ask questions and explore ideas, allowing students to collaborate and share their expertise, developing learning strategies to cope with complex and challenging material and lessons, and offering opportunities for students to realign the task to their personal interests, facilitating internalisation and self-management of learning. The cognitive component is essential for increasing learners' involvement, motivation, and engagement in learning. Student ownership of learning can be promoted by creating opportunities for learners/teachers to:

- Discuss multiple approaches and strategies
- Find multiple solutions to problems
- Justify solutions for the purpose of sharing expertise
- Have ample time for decision making
- Solve learning problems independently
- Re-evaluate errors
- Provide informational feedback
- Formulate personal goals or realign tasks to correspond with interest

- Debate ideas freely
- Reduce teacher talk time and increase teacher listening time
- Ask questions

Stefanou et al. (2004) argue for a more inclusive conception of autonomy, which involves cognitive choices as well as procedural and organizational ones. In order for such choices to be possible, learners need to develop and sustain their sometimes fragile identity as learners (Lamb, 2011) by, for example, having the opportunity to reflect critically on existing learner beliefs and to develop their metacognitive knowledge (Lamb, 2005b, 2006, 2011). Stefanou et al. (2004) further suggest that it is *cognitive autonomy support* that truly leads to the psychological investment in learning that educators strive for. Relying exclusively on organizational and procedural autonomy support may not develop intrinsic motivation. Choice and decision making are, obviously, crucial to foster engagement in learning but cognitive autonomy support is probably the fundamental ingredient without which motivation and engagement may not be maximized (Stefanou et al., 2004). It is agreed that it fosters a more lasting psychological investment in deep-level thinking.

Autonomy support is essentially about creating conditions for autonomy to flourish, and it requires teachers to develop knowledge about the students, flexibility, willingness to share control, and a dialogical approach to teaching.

Engagement and intrinsic motivation

The creation of an atmosphere where learners *feel motivated to learn* is central to effective learning. Engagement refers to a learner's active involvement in learning activities, that is, the extent to which learning has actually become a true priority for them. School learning requires commitment and effort, so engagement is absolutely crucial. It is usually regarded as the first step on the route to motivation and, according to Fredricks, Blumenfeld & Paris (2004), a crucial factor in learners' school success. Newmann (1989: 34) defined engagement as "psychological investment", entailing connection, attachment and integration. In contrast, disengagement means isolation, separation, detachment and fragmentation, but the opposite of engagement is disaffection, which refers to the existence of behaviours and emotions that reflect maladaptive motivational states. Dis-affection with school leads to passivity, withdrawal from participation in learning activities, boredom, frustration in the classroom and, sometimes, anti-social behaviour.

In a school context, engagement combines a behavioural and an emotional dimension and refers to "active, goal-directed, flexible, constructive, persistent, focused, emotionally positive interactions with the social and physical environments" (Skinner et al., 2008: 766). For Shulman (2002), engagement is the fundamental purpose of education. Engaged students are actively involved and attentive in class, participating in learning activities, asking questions, responding to comments, etc. In addition, engagement empowers students, provides them with choices, and encourages students to be pro-active on their own initiative. Garret (2011) proposes some strategies for promoting student engagement:

- Show your own engagement and emphasize that you value engagement
- Ask students about their definitions of engagement and how it relates to learning
- Give students a variety of options to show their engagement
- Ask learners to periodically reflect and report on their engagement
- Create memorable moments
- Involve learners in designing creative class activities
- Solicit feedback from learners to identify significant activities that were engaging

Some researchers have described what may be referred to as *pedagogies of engagement* (Barnett & Coate, 2005; Edgerton, 2001), that is, those pedagogies where teaching is understood as engaging learners in learning, giving them the space and the time in which they can flourish. For Barnett & Coate (2005: 148), a pedagogy of engagement is one of

> (…) deep and abiding respect for each student, of generosity and of space and time. It is a pedagogy in which the students are enabled to develop a strong voice, but a voice that is responsive to others and the challenges and standards inherent in the experiences opened up.

These pedagogies not only increase learners' active engagement in learning and academic work but also enhance cognitive and psychosocial change (Pascarella & Terenzini, 1991). Umbach & Wawrzynski (2005) found higher levels of engagement and learning in lessons where the teacher uses active and collaborative learning techniques, engages students in relevant learning experiences, emphasizes higher-order cognitive activities in the classroom, interacts with students, and challenges them academically. Learners do value enriching educational experiences. Furthermore, engagement develops in classrooms that support autonomy in contrast with control-oriented ones.

As for motivation, it is a complex, multifaceted concept that has occupied a central role in discussions of teaching. However, motivation is not something that you do to learners. From our perspective, it is crucial to be aware that what the teacher can do is create the conditions for it to flourish. The relationship between autonomy and motivation is a complex one. Self-determination theory maintains that human motivation is dependent on the presence of three basic psychological needs: autonomy, competence, and relatedness. The need for autonomy refers to the need for agency and responsibility over school work, and the need to feel a sense of full volition and agency regarding one's activities and goals, a feeling that emerges when one's actions and goals are experienced as emanating from one's authentic self (Deci & Ryan, 1985). The need for relatedness refers to the need to feel closely related to other people and the need for competence is the need to be effective in one's interactions with the environment, and to feel that one is capable of mastering challenges (Deci & Ryan, 1985, 2000).

Although various factors are essential to intrinsic motivation, perceived autonomy has been shown to be a necessary condition, and extrinsic rewards run a serious risk of diminishing autonomy and intrinsic motivation (Deci, Koestner & Ryan, 1999). Motivation to learn is also about dispositions which represent *readiness to act in a given direction*. Examples of dispositions are trust, readiness to listen, attentiveness, self-appraisal, and willingness to assume responsibility. These are all dispositions that as teachers we want to foster in our students to make their learning more effective. Among the factors that promote intrinsic motivation we find: challenge, control, responsibility, curiosity, fantasy, cooperation, and recognition. Teacher *feedback* also seems to represent a decisive factor for effective motivational thinking, as long as it promotes internal belief structures and attributional processes that optimize learner involvement (Ushioda, 1996) and is 'informational' rather than 'controlling' (Deci & Porac, 1978: 162).

The development of autonomy is itself a stimulus for the development of motivation (Lamb, 2003, 2004).

The degree to which learners experience autonomy in learning is closely related to the quality of their engagement and intrinsic motivation. Therefore, promoting engagement and motivation is a basic principle of pedagogy for autonomy.

Learner differentiation

Research has shown that individuals differ in many ways which *affect learning* (e.g. Skehan, 1989). Learners differ in their interests, attitudes, knowledge base, learning and cognitive styles, learning strategies and rhythm, prior knowledge, motivation, and affective idiosyncrasies. These learner differences give rise to distinct learning and curriculum requirements, hence their relevance for instruction. However, teachers tend to develop a particular picture of their individual learners, which focuses on only one or two of their attributes (such as ability, behaviour, motivation) (Cooper & McIntyre, 1996; Hargreaves, Hester & Mellor, 1975). Of course some of these differences affect foreign language learning more than others, but it is important that language teachers should become more aware of them and find ways of teaching that cater to the different individual needs. In this sense, Hedge (2000) holds that there is no direct relationship between teaching and learning. This makes it almost impossible for a teacher to set the same learning objectives for a class and expect all learners to attain them uniformly. Rather it is far more appropriate for the teacher to make content available to learners, so that they can work on it in different ways and at their own rhythms and accept that the degree of mastery achieved will vary across learners. Indeed, learners usually learn much more than teachers intend.

Accommodating teaching to such learner differences is one of the most fundamental challenges of education. Teachers can encourage differentiation at two levels: (a) school level, that is, supporting ability grouping strategies, and (b) classroom level, that is, making use of differentiated instruction strategies to enhance learning by matching instruction and assessment to student characteristics. Even though differentiation is not easy to achieve in classrooms where teachers work with large classes, it is precisely in these classrooms that it is more necessary, not only to accommodate and foster learning diversity, but also to allow learners to develop the self-regulation abilities that enable them to become more independent in a formal collective environment. Practical examples and proposals regarding differentiation (e.g. Convery & Coyle, 1999; Jiménez Raya & Lamb, 2003) suggest that it is possible to effectively differentiate curriculum processes by encouraging:

- *Higher levels of thinking and reflection.* Pedagogy should stress use rather than acquisition of information; students should apply information to new situations, use it to develop new ideas, and evaluate its appropriateness. Learning tasks should include a greater percentage of open ones – those for which there is no predetermined right answer and which stimulate further interaction, thinking, and research.
- *Freedom of choice.* Learners should be given freedom to choose, when possible, what to learn and how to study in order to increase their interest in learning, because allowing learners the freedom to be who they really are engenders greater responsibility for self-directed action (Deci & Flaste 1995: 72). Personalization and choice contribute to a differentiated environment.
- *Cooperative learning.* Cooperation facilitates the accommodation of the curriculum to different individual factors because learners will support and help each other. Cooperative learning permits learners to work at different levels of complexity and at their own pace (see McCafferty, Jacobs & Iddings, 2006; Nunan, 1992).
- *Discovery and enquiry.* Enquiry characteristically refers to both the process of seeking knowledge and new insight as well as to a method of teaching. Enquiry learning promotes the improvement of the processes and enabling skills usually involved in forming concepts and facts, supporting learners in the process of becoming researchers and lifelong learners. As a teaching approach enquiry aims to develop enquirers and to encourage them to use curiosity, that is, the urge to explore and to understand, as motivating factors leading to learning through personal engagement.
- *Experiential learning.* The goal of experiential learning is to encourage learners to use the target language in new situations, use it to develop new ideas, evaluate its appropriateness, and to create new meanings. This

approach takes into account differences in learning ability, and is responsive both to learners' needs and practical pedagogical considerations. In experiential learning, learning tasks are expected to include a higher proportion of situations in which learners are encouraged to use their inductive reasoning processes to discover patterns, ideas and underlying principles. It involves: (1) creating a positive atmosphere for learning, (2) making learning objectives clear, (3) fostering the participation of learners in the learning process and supporting them in gaining control over its nature and direction, (4) balancing intellectual and emotional components of learning, sharing feelings and thoughts with learners, an openness to change, (5) creating opportunities for learners to experiment with practical, social and research problems, and (6) organizing and making available learning resources (see Kohonen et al., 2001).

- *Pacing, variety and variable teacher support.* Teachers need to pace material or negotiate learning pace with learners as a differentiation strategy. The use of a variety of methods maintains learners' interest and accommodates different learning styles, too. Concerning support, differentiation can be achieved by providing different kinds and degrees of support to individual learners.

Differentiated instruction is inextricably linked to a continuous and individualised evaluation of learners' progress and difficulties in learning. It is essential in learning-centred pedagogies and it can be implemented to different degrees depending on contextual variables.

Action-orientedness

Cognitive learning theory holds that learning is an active, self-constructed, and intentional process (Bereiter & Scardamalia, 1989; Jonassen, 1991a/b; Simons, 1992). Furthermore, psychological theories of human agency (Bandura, 2001) emphasise that people are not just on-looking hosts of internal mechanisms orchestrated by environmental events. On the contrary, people are *agents of experiences* rather than simply undergoing experiences. Agency implies voice, feeling that one is in control of one's own actions. This perspective is in tune with an *action-oriented approach* in language education as proposed in the Common European Framework of Reference for Languages (Council of Europe, 2001a), which involves learners in performing a wide variety of purposeful *tasks* whereby they develop academic and learning competences, apply language processes to produce and/or receive texts in relation to themes in specific domains, activate relevant strategies, and monitor and assess their learning. Learners are regarded mostly as 'social agents', that is, members of society who have tasks to do under particular circumstances, in a specific environment and within a particular field of action. Therefore, the action-based approach is said to exploit the cognitive, emotional and volitional resources and the full range of abilities specific to and applied by the individual as a social agent. Action-oriented teaching as an approach places human agency in the centre of the process.

In the language classroom an action-oriented approach can be enacted through task-based language teaching (TBLT), which is a strong version of the communicative approach. It can be described as a 'holistic' approach "which attempts to integrate all aspects of language, language use and learning into a comprehensive pedagogy" so that "learners are able to experience the TL [target language] as a purposeful and user-sensitive system, providing a reference point for whatever analytical language work might be wanted, whether phonological, lexical, grammatical or pragmatic" (Bygate, 2015: 16). It can be implemented in various ways provided that the main focus is on meaning and that language instruction is planned so as to support communicative needs (see Ellis, 2003; Nunan, 2004; Willis, 1996). TBLT is based on the assumption that "language learning will progress most successfully if teaching aims simply to create contexts in which the learner's natural language learning capacity can be nurtured rather than making a systematic attempt to teach the language bit by bit" (Ellis, 2009: 222). This assumption goes counter to mainstream understandings of language education. Most language programmes are not based on a task-based rationale, but teachers can nevertheless develop a 'task-supported' approach that complements the prescribed curriculum (East, 2015). Ellis (2003: 276–278) proposes a set of eight methodological principles that can guide TBLT:

- Ensure an appropriate level of task difficulty
- Establish clear goals for each task-based lesson
- Develop an appropriate orientation to performing the task in the students
- Ensure that students adopt an active role in task-based lessons
- Encourage students to take risks

- Ensure that students are primarily focused on meaning when they perform a task
- Provide opportunities for focusing on form
- Require students to evaluate their performance and progress

TBLT can promote learners' autonomy as language users by enhancing communicative language use, language awareness, and the ability to assess performance and progress.

Conversational interaction

Pedagogy for autonomy has implications for classroom discourse. In traditional language classrooms, the teacher often decides who talks to whom, about what and how, which results in the students' loss of initiative and control in regard to discourse. One of the goals of pedagogy for autonomy is to *enhance discourse power* as learners engage in meaningful interactions among themselves and with the teacher. This involves achieving greater interactional *symmetry* among *unequal* participants. Van Lier (1996) discusses the possibility of moving from transmission-oriented communication to transformation-oriented communication through changing the nature of interaction. In conversational interaction, participants negotiate the pedagogical agenda and co-construct meanings and events so as to build a more democratic environment where communication becomes exploratory and contingent on everyone's expectations, interests, and concerns. Contingent utterances relate new material to known material and set up expectancies for what may come next, thus being never entirely predictable or unpredictable and promoting intersubjectivity and continued attention (ibid: 184). Exploring transformation-oriented classroom discourse entails "a dynamic tension between diversity and homogeneity, between many voices and one voice, between autonomy and external control, between conversation and monolog" (ibid.: 183).

Low levels of mastery of the foreign language are a constraint to conversational interaction and can become an impediment to verbal reflection on language and the learning process. Pedagogy for autonomy requires teachers to determine the circumstances where the mother tongue can become an *empowering instrument*, and its use must be carefully and intentionally planned. Refusing to use the mother tongue on the grounds of hindering foreign language learning, might turn the foreign language itself into a deskilling tool. This is a controversial issue that requires thoughtful consideration and more investigation in both monolingual and multilingual classroom settings.

Fostering conversational interaction in the language classroom is a way to increase communication on whatever topic is being dealt with. It involves seeing the classroom as a real-world context where teachers and learners express personal meaning, negotiate understandings, and build pedagogy together.

Reflective enquiry

Reflection is a central concept in educational theory. It is often argued that reflection is another word for thinking. According to Mezirow, the transformation of our frames of reference takes place through *"critical reflection on the assumptions* upon which our interpretations, beliefs, and habits of mind or points of view are based" (Mezirow, 1997: 7). This principle includes the possibility of involving learners as partners of teacher-led enquiry, as well as the need to provide them with opportunities to analyse their learning experience themselves. Reflective enquiry is, in fact, essential for learner development, and it enhances teacher knowledge of the learners, which, in turn, should result in an improved teaching-learning process.

Reflection has been found to play an important role in getting individuals to reorganise or restructure their knowledge (Jiménez Raya, 1997, 2002). It is crucial to give students opportunities to think about their learning process so that they can become aware of their own beliefs and how what they do to facilitate language acquisition is influenced by those beliefs (Jiménez Raya, 2006). Reflection is also central to learning because understanding is more likely to occur when a student is required to explain, elaborate, or defend his or her position. Having to explain one's position/actions can often be the stimulus needed to make learners evaluate and elaborate knowledge in new ways, causing them to assimilate new information and restructure prior conceptions (Brown & Campione, 1986). Learner reflection in language learning, according to Jiménez Raya (2013), is directly related to elements that are essential to autonomy, cognitive development and meaningful learning such as:

- The development of metacognition, that is, the capacity for learners to improve their ability to think about their thinking;
- The development of critical thinking, problem solving, and the capacity for learners to engage in higher-level thinking skills;
- The ability to self-evaluate, that is, the capacity for students to judge the quality of their work based on evidence and explicit criteria for the purpose of improving.

Concerning the teacher, if pedagogy for autonomy is to become mainstream in language teaching, there is a pressing need for *teacher-led reflective enquiry through experimentation* so that new insights and ideas can be derived from practice. Reflective teachers, according to Zeichner & Liston (1996):

- examine, frame and attempt to solve the dilemmas of classroom practice;
- are aware of and question the assumptions and values they bring to teaching;
- are attentive to the institutional and cultural contexts in which they teach;
- take part in curriculum development and are involved in school change efforts;
- take responsibility for their own professional development.

The need for reflective enquiry has implications for teacher development programmes, where conditions should be created for teachers to develop a critical understanding of language education, enquire into their own theories and practices, uncover and challenge situational constraints, develop self-determined action plans, engage in professional dialogue with others, evaluate learning processes and outcomes, and participate in the dissemination of pedagogical experiences (Vieira, 2003, 2006; Vieira et al., 2010; Jiménez Raya & Vieira, 2015). How teacher education might promote pedagogy for autonomy will be the topic of the following chapter.

Reflective enquiry undertaken by either teachers or learners can be greatly facilitated by reflective dialogue, a conversation with oneself and others about teaching and/or learning processes, which can take place orally or in written form. Teaching and learning portfolios, journals and other reflective records are especially useful here, as they provide a space for systematic reflective accounts of teaching and learning experience, thus also providing data that can help us understand the nature and impact of teaching and learning practices.

Formative assessment, assessment for learning and assessment for autonomy

Quite paradoxically, recognising that education is a human right and that educational systems must be decentralised so as to respond to local needs has reinforced (inter)national standardised testing as a means of ensuring that everyone has access to quality education and that education quality is equivalent across educational communities (Smith, 2016: 12–13). A 'global testing culture' has grown in a vast number of countries worldwide, emphasising standardised, high-stakes assessment for measuring the efficiency of schools and educational systems, and leading to "an environment where testing becomes synonymous with accountability, which becomes synonymous with quality" (ibid.: 7).

However, a primary focus on testing for accountability purposes reduces assessment diversity and has a negative impact on the role of assessment for *learning*. If we accept that the central goal of teaching is to understand and enhance learning, then assessment must be context-sensitive and learning-oriented. This means that *formative assessment* should occupy a central role in teaching: "Assessment is to be seen as a moment of learning, and students have to be active in their own assessment and to picture their own learning in the light of an understanding of what it means to get better" (Black & Wiliam, 1998: 30).

Formative assessment can be broadly defined "an ongoing process of gathering information on the extent of learning, on strengths and weaknesses, which the teachers can feedback into their course planning and the actual feedback they give learners" (Council of Europe, 2001a: 186). It involves a diversification of assessment instruments beyond tests (e.g. checklists, questionnaires, learning logs and journals, and portfolios), and an integrated focus on students' communicative and learning competences, in the latter case involving three dimensions of learning (Vieira & Moreira, 1993: 71): *the learner's self* (e.g. personal attitudes, styles and preferences), *the learning processes* (e.g. difficulties and strategies in reading), and *the didactic processes* (e.g. teaching strategies and materials).

Formative assessment is assessment for and as learning, requiring a culturally-responsive classroom environment of equality and mutuality where learners understand what they are learning and what they are expected to learn, receive constructive feedback on their work and advice on how to improve it, participate in decision-making on what to do next and know how to get support, build metacognitive knowledge about themselves and learning tasks, and take responsibility for learning (Clark, 2011: 163). Actually, feedback only works if students are in a position to notice, receive, interpret and integrate the information they receive, and this "implies self-direction, which implies training towards self-direction, monitoring one's learning, and developing ways of action on feedback" (Council of Europe, 2001a: 186). Self-/peer-assessment is therefore intrinsic to formative assessment. In this type of assessment, "value is placed on the students' personal beliefs, opinions, guesses and misconceptions", and "when students are permitted to express who they are, they develop a strong sense of self-efficacy, a central requirement for autonomous learning strategies" (Clark, 2011: 171). Given the close relationship between assessment for learning and learner autonomy and the need to enhance autonomy, "it would be necessary to encourage [learners] to articulate not only what they have learnt, but also how they learned it, their own role in that learning, and how they may enhance that role" (Lamb & Little, 2016: 188). This has led to the notion of "assessment for autonomy" (Lamb, 2010a), where the purpose "would not be to measure autonomy for its own sake, with a view to defining levels of ability or ranking pupils, but to increase learners' self-awareness of their own autonomy and teachers' awareness of what constitutes such autonomy and how they may adapt their teaching in order to enhance it" (Lamb, 2010a: 101).

For the reasons pointed out above, formative assessment is a crucial principle of pedagogy for autonomy and is closely connected with other principles, namely the promotion of responsibility and flexible control, learning to learn and self-regulation, autonomy support, engagement and intrinsic motivation, learner differentiation, conversational interaction, and reflective enquiry. In providing invaluable information on students' communicative and learning competences, formative assessment helps language teachers adjust teaching to local learning needs and can become a powerful driver of curriculum development and innovation (see Costa & Kallick,

2004; Rea-Dickins & Germaine, 1992). Promoting formative assessment in an era of expanding accountability assessment is thus necessary if schools are to become more humanistic and democratic settings.

4.3 Beyond formulae: a situated view of pedagogy for autonomy

The pedagogical principles sketched in the section above should allow teachers to develop their autonomy as professionals, as it requires them to assume responsibility for determining "what specific route they have to follow, what treacherous curves they have to negotiate, what institutional speed bumps they have to surmount, and what unexpected detours they have to take" (Kumaravadivelu, 2001: 551). Obviously, all these decisions will depend on the landscape in which their everyday teaching occurs.

We now invite you to use the table below to reflect on your current teaching priorities and possible future changes as regards the principles we propose. Note that, due to our parallel focus on teacher and learner autonomy, the principles apply also to teacher development. Therefore, you can also ask similar questions about the extent to which teacher development approaches foster teacher-as-learner autonomy.

- Is this principle a priority for me as a teacher?
- If it is, why is it a priority and how do I address it?
- If not, should/could it be made more explicit and intentional in my practice?
- If so, why and how should/could it be made more explicit and intentional in my practice?

Table 7. Reflection on principles of pedagogy for autonomy

Pedagogical principles	*Are they part of my teaching priorities? Why (not)? If so, how?*	*Should they be made more intentional in my practice? Why (not)? If so, how?*
Responsibility, choice, and flexible control	Yes ☐ No ☐	Yes ☐ No ☐
Learning to learn and self-regulation	Yes ☐ No ☐	Yes ☐ No ☐

Pedagogical principles	Are they part of my teaching priorities? Why (not)? If so, how?	Should they be made more intentional in my practice? Why (not)? If so, how?
Integration and explicitness	Yes ☐ No ☐	Yes ☐ No ☐
Autonomy support	Yes ☐ No ☐	Yes ☐ No ☐
Engagement and intrinsic motivation	Yes ☐ No ☐	Yes ☐ No ☐
Learner differentiation	Yes ☐ No ☐	Yes ☐ No ☐
Action-orientedness	Yes ☐ No ☐	Yes ☐ No ☐
Conversational interaction	Yes ☐ No ☐	Yes ☐ No ☐
Reflective enquiry	Yes ☐ No ☐	Yes ☐ No ☐
Formative assessment, assessment for learning and assessment for autonomy	Yes ☐ No ☐	Yes ☐ No ☐

According to Jiménez Raya & Vieira (2011), developing pedagogy for autonomy can be like doing a jigsaw-puzzle. It involves working with a large number of pieces that only start making sense as we begin to assemble them, trying to discover which fit which, constructing, deconstructing and reconstructing images, tentatively and attentively, patiently and persistently... This means that we need to move beyond seeking teaching formulae and embrace a situated view of pedagogy for autonomy. Usually, pedagogy for autonomy entails the creation of an atmosphere of freedom in the classroom that allows learners and teacher to explore learning possibilities in collaboration. Approaches to pedagogy for autonomy or pedagogies for autonomy have followed two main traditions (Jiménez Raya & Lamb, 2008b: 64): one that focuses on the enhancement of learner control over different learning decisions (flexible learning, project work, independent learning...), and the other centring on internal factors that influence learners toward accepting responsibility and controlling their thoughts and actions as learners (learning to learn, self-regulated learning, strategy training...). Nevertheless, both approaches to pedagogy for autonomy can be, indeed need to be, combined. Whatever the approach adopted it will empower learners, fostering a sense of agency that will transfer beyond the classroom, encouraging learners to participate in meaningful educational experiences, explore more effective ways of learning from which they can profit, monitor their progress toward their goals, make adjustments in their efforts when necessary, and establish new and more ambitious goals as they attain previous ones.

Because there is no simple formula for the promotion of learner autonomy in language teaching methodology, we want to stress the fact that teachers can actually create conditions in their classrooms that allow for learner and teacher development. As we have said before, even in the most adverse circumstances *every teacher can do something*. It is just a question of navigating the space of possibility, what can actually be. Our suggestion throughout this volume is that we should critically analyse language education *as it is* and seek new opportunities to develop it *as it can be*, based on an ideal view of *what it should be*. Our struggle ought to be about developing context-sensitive, re[ide]alistic practices that can support new powerful forms of teaching and learning to serve levels of expectation higher than anything imagined in the past. To this end, it is crucial to understand the rationale for the promotion of pedagogy for autonomy as well as what it entails. This book is driven by the belief that only in such an educational framework can pervasive, authentic, inquisitive and reflective learning and teaching be constructed. Figure 2 summarises that framework, according to which mapping pedagogy for autonomy implies a consideration of *context, learner* and *teacher* variables, as well as the development of pedagogical principles that may challenge and transform existing traditions and enhance an empowering view of education.

Figure 2. Pedagogy for autonomy framework

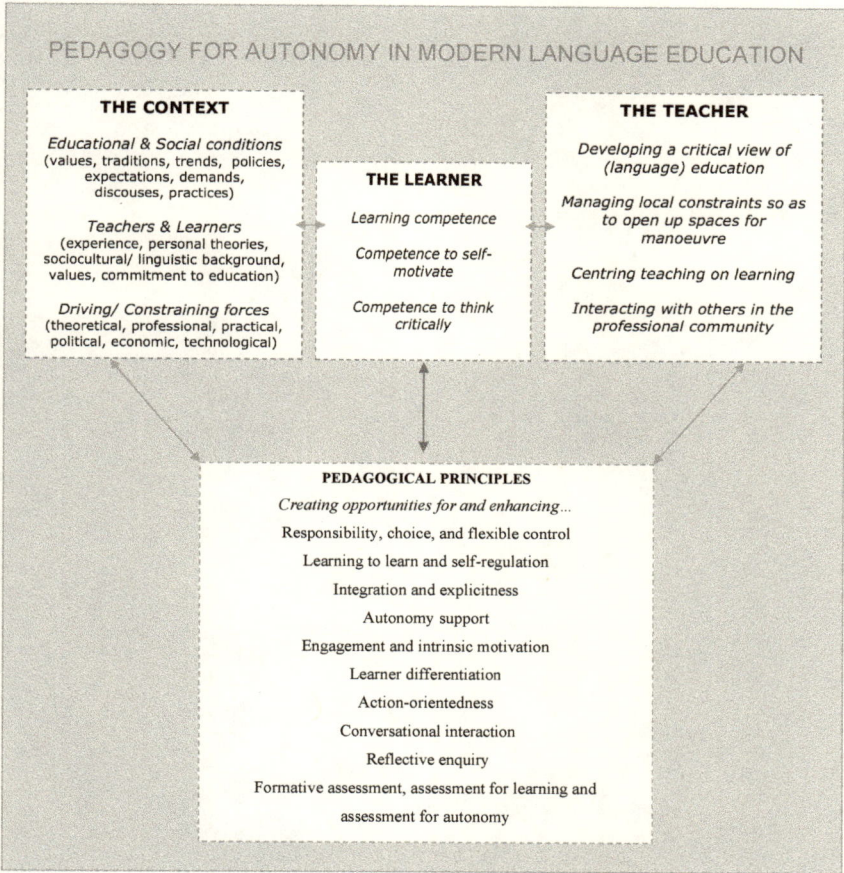

PEDAGOGY FOR AUTONOMY IN MODERN LANGUAGE EDUCATION

THE CONTEXT

Educational & Social conditions
(values, traditions, trends, policies, expectations, demands, discouses, practices)

Teachers & Learners
(experience, personal theories, sociocultural/ linguistic background, values, commitment to education)

Driving/ Constraining forces
(theoretical, professional, practical, political, economic, technological)

THE LEARNER

Learning competence

Competence to self-motivate

Competence to think critically

THE TEACHER

Developing a critical view of (language) education

Managing local constraints so as to open up spaces for manoeuvre

Centring teaching on learning

Interacting with others in the professional community

PEDAGOGICAL PRINCIPLES

Creating opportunities for and enhancing...

Responsibility, choice, and flexible control

Learning to learn and self-regulation

Integration and explicitness

Autonomy support

Engagement and intrinsic motivation

Learner differentiation

Action-orientedness

Conversational interaction

Reflective enquiry

Formative assessment, assessment for learning and assessment for autonomy

5. Teacher education for autonomy – An experience-oriented approach

The promotion of pedagogy for autonomy in language education requires pre- and in-service teacher education programmes to provide (prospective) teachers with opportunities to experience autonomy both as *learners of teaching* and as *teachers of learning*. Even though accounts of autonomy-oriented programmes and projects are presented in the literature (see reviews undertaken by Benson, 2011; Jiménez Raya & Vieira, 2008; Manzano Vázquez, 2016), there is no evidence to suggest that autonomy has become a priority in language teacher education. Moreover, popular language teacher training coursebooks appear to contain little or no information about it (Reinders & Balcikanli, 2011).

Teacher education for autonomy has implications for teacher development strategies, and the purpose of this chapter is to offer some ideas on what can be done. Although there are plenty of strategies that can be used, we will focus on *case pedagogy* as an experience-oriented approach that can empower teachers to understand and explore pedagogy for autonomy as they become enquiry-oriented professionals.

5.1 Reflective teacher education for autonomy

Despite current developments in the teacher education field, teacher education strategies often rely on a theory-to-practice rationale that reflects, to a large extent, the prevalence of a positivistic epistemology characterised as 'instrumental rationalism', according to which teachers are seen more as technicians than as critical intellectuals, curriculum developers, and agents of change (Kincheloe, 2003). In order to be empowering, teacher education must challenge this tradition, inspiring and preparing teachers to become empowering educators. Empowerment in education presupposes a critical-democratic pedagogy for personal and social change, in which the goals are "to relate personal growth to public life, by developing strong skills, academic knowledge, habits of enquiry, and critical curiosity about society, power, inequality, and change" (Shor, 1992: 15). Through this process educational actors and organizations "learn to critically appropriate knowledge existing outside their immediate experience in order to broaden their understanding of themselves, the world, and the possibilities for transforming the taken-for-granted assumptions about the way we live" (MacLaren, 1989: 186).

In the late 20th century, proposals for 'reflective teacher education' have emerged, highlighting the need for teachers to become critical enquirers and stressing the centrality of experience for professional renewal and empowerment (e.g. Schön, 1987; Smyth 1987, 1989; Tabachnick & Zeichner, 1991; Tom 1985; Zeichner, 1983; Zeichner & Liston, 1996). Nevertheless, there has been a lot of variation in how institutions organise and develop teacher education programmes, and teacher educators hold different positions about what learning to teach means, making it impossible to reach a common agreement about the role of teacher education vis-à-vis school cultures (Zeichner & Conklin, 2008). A central issue here is: *should teacher education adjust to or transform existing teaching cultures?*

It is a fact that many teacher educators "counteridentify with school teaching as currently practiced (and with schools as currently constituted)", thus hoping to "transform occupational competence against the weight of conventional practice and the circumstances of teaching in the schools" (Sykes, Bird & Kennedy, 2010: 468). However, in seeking to transform the realities of schooling, training institutions have often adopted a superior stance that relates to how workplaces have been historically understood in professional development. As Bohlinger et al. (2015) point out, the progressive degradation of work as a site of learning in modern industrial societies, along with an over-rating of formal education and credentials, have contributed to the academisation of professional learning and affected the content of learning and the epistemology of knowledge: "Learning of standardised, codified and abstract knowledge *for work* in educational institutions has displaced the learning of situated, specific and embodied knowledge *in work*" (Bohlinger et al., 2015: 224).

Reflective teacher education entails not only the adoption of reflective strategies but also the development of collegial relationships between academic teacher educators and teachers, as well as a dynamic interplay between 'knowledge for work' and 'knowledge in work', the latter referring to the construction of context-sensitive practical knowledge and wisdom on the basis of pedagogical experimentation and enquiry, namely through action research processes (Leitch & Day, 2000; Lunenberg & Korthagen, 2009; Vaughan & Burnaford, 2016). *Experiential pedagogies* are thus needed in teacher education settings so as to enhance a praxeological epistemology, allowing teachers to theorise from practice with a transformative purpose and facilitating the construction of personal theories and practices that are conceptually and ethically sound, locally valid and socially relevant (Vieira, 2014a/b). As we suggested before, dealing with complexity and uncertainty in educational settings is integral to 're[ide]alistic' professional lifelong learning and pedagogies, that is, transformation takes place between reality and ideals.

In experiential pedagogies, teachers are encouraged to engage in self-directed professional learning, both individually and with others (students, peers, mentors…), by analysing their own interests and needs, establishing goals and plans, and monitoring and evaluating their development. Richards & Farrell (2005: 14) suggest that self-directed professional learning involves the following processes:

- *Enquiry*. Asking questions about one's own teaching practices and seeking information needed to answer these questions.
- *Self-appraisal*. Assessing one's teaching and development on the basis of evidence from oneself and others and the ability to critically reflect with the desire to analyse oneself in order to determine one's strengths and weaknesses.
- *Experience*. Personal experience becomes the basis and stimulus for learning.
- *Personal construction*. Meaning is personally constructed by the teacher as learner.
- *Planning and managing*. Learning is dependent on the ability to set short- and long-term goals and to select strategies for their achievement.

Teacher development can be pursued in many different ways as indicated in Table 8, based on Richards & Farrell (2005).

Table 8. Teacher development activities (Richards & Farrell, 2005)

INDIVIDUAL	ONE-TO-ONE	GROUP-BASED	INSTITUTIONAL
Self-monitoring Journal writing Critical incidents Teaching portfolios Action research	Peer coaching Peer observation Critical friendships Action research Critical incidents Team teaching	Case studies Action research Journal writing Teacher support groups	Workshops Action research Teacher support groups

According to Jiménez Raya & Vieira (2011: 22), teacher development activities can help teachers develop their competence to promote pedagogy for autonomy by helping them…

- Uncover their pedagogical beliefs, values, priorities, dilemmas, concerns…
- Document their practice and reflect on its conceptual, practical and social justifications
- Question the implications of their practice for the development of learner autonomy
- Be sensitive to their students' beliefs, values, priorities, dilemmas, concerns…
- Look at pedagogical problems as starting points for enquiry
- Take an exploratory approach to teaching with a focus on learning
- Collect student data to assess the quality of teaching and learning processes
- Be attentive to how contexts of practice foster or hinder their own and their students' autonomy
- Find strategies to manage constraints on autonomy
- Learn to deal with the complexity, uniqueness and indeterminacy of pedagogical situations
- Enter communities of practice where collaboration and dialogue sustain individual and collective efforts to promote autonomy

In the following section we focus on *case pedagogy* in teacher education, which emphasises the experiential nature of teacher learning and has the potential to fulfil all the purposes above.

5.2 Case pedagogy for promoting learner and teacher autonomy

Case methods in teacher education have been proposed as a way to enhance the experiential basis of professional learning. The underlying assumption is that teachers' stories of teaching can provide the basis for professional reflection and enquiry (see Clandinin, 2007). Because cases are situated episodes of real practice, they can present a complex picture of educational experience and convey the idea that teaching requires the exercise of critical thinking and judgement. According to Shulman (2004a: 543–544),

> Cases are ways of parsing experience so practitioners can examine and learn from it. Case methods thus become strategies for helping professionals "chunk" their experience into units that can become the focus for reflective practice. Cases therefore can become the basis for individual professional learning as well as a forum within which communities of professionals (…) can store, exchange and organize their experiences. They may well become, for teacher education, the lingua franca of teacher learning communities.

A case-based pedagogy requires the analysis or the production of professional narratives conceptualised as *cases*. Shulman (2004b: 474) contends that "to assert that a narrative is a *case* is to engage in an act of theory": it requires teachers to connect the narrative to personal/other experiences, that is, to other cases, and also to "categories of experience, to theoretical classifications through which they organise and make sense of their world". Therefore, "every case, in its particularity, derives its 'case-ness' from its connections to other cases and to organizing principles or theories" (ibid.: 479).

In reading or writing narratives of enquiry into experience, teachers may reconstruct their professional thinking and action. Narrative enquiry can strengthen teachers' situated reflective learning, practice and professional identities in an authentic manner, opening up the possibility to develop a *standpoint* from *within* the world in which they live as a way of empowering them to transform that world (Doecke, 2013). Johnson & Golombek (2002) underline the role of narrative enquiry *for* and *as* professional development:

> Through inquiry, teachers frame and reframe the issues and problems they face in their professional worlds. As teachers engage in narrative inquiry, they become theorizers in their own right, and as theorizers, they look less for certain answers

and more to rethink what they thought they already knew. Thus, we believe that teachers' stories of inquiry are not only *about* professional development; they *are* professional development. Narrative inquiry becomes a means through which teachers actualize their ways of knowing and growing that nourish and sustain their professional development throughout their careers. (Johnson & Golombek, 2002: 6)

Three different strategies based on Jiménez Raya & Vieira (2011, 2015) are proposed here for a case-based approach in teacher education for autonomy, although they can be combined:

Teachers analyse cases of other teachers' experience
Teachers develop and write cases from their own experience
Teacher educators write cases from teachers' experience

In all three strategies, cases are based on real autonomy-oriented teacher experience and should illustrate at least some of the pedagogical principles set out in chapter 4 above. It is expected that by analysing and/or building case narratives, teachers will become more aware of what pedagogy for autonomy entails and also more willing and able to experiment with it. Finally, it is important to point out that case pedagogy requires the fulfilment of the following conditions (Jiménez Raya & Vieira, 2015: 103):

- Use and production of cases that are thought-provoking and can be related to relevant professional experience and theoretical ideas
- Time to explore cases in different directions, using multiple frames of reference
- Expanded contextual and theoretical knowledge to analyse complex educational phenomena
- Articulation of the uniqueness of educational experience with general concepts and principles
- Ability to integrate theory and practice in a rather unpredictable, flexible way
- Ability to conduct a reflective, dialogical approach in the construction of professional knowledge
- Creativity and ingenuity as regards generating and evaluating innovative practices
- Development of enquiry and writing competences (attitudes, knowledge, abilities)

5.2.1 Analysing cases of other teachers' experience

The analysis of teaching cases written by others is the most common strategy found in the literature on case pedagogy. According to Shulman (1992), the interpretation of cases as illustrations of professional practice allows teachers to explore classroom strategies but also theoretical principles and ethical aspects of teaching. It further allows them to build images of the possible, provided that cases illustrate innovative approaches. In order for case analysis to promote pedagogy for autonomy, cases must account for autonomy-oriented language teaching experiences. These can be found in the autonomy literature, but if teacher educators also ask teachers to produce case narratives (see 5.2.2 below), then it is possible for them to collect cases over time and use them for case analysis (see Vieira, 2014a).

As Shulman (2004b) points out, case analysis emerges from a central question – *what is this a case of?* It is this question that allows teachers to (re)interpret the case and learn from it:

> (...) the key move made in teaching with cases occurs when instructor and students explore the question, "what is this a case of?". As they wrestle with this question, they move the case in two directions simultaneously. They connect this narrative to their remembered (personal) experiences or to vicariously experienced cases written or recounted by others, thus relating this particular case to other specific cases. They also connect this narrative to categories of experience, to theoretical classifications through which they organise and make sense of their world. (Shulman, 2004b: 474)

However, as Shulman also points out, the richness and complexity of educational experience requires multiple answers to that question, that is, "rarely if ever is a particular account related to only one theoretical, conceptual or descriptive category. Indeed, part of the power of cases rests in a given case's capacity to be related to multiple categories and to numerous other instances" (Shulman, 2004b: 467). This means that the analysis of cases requires the use of multiple frames of reference.

How teacher educators provoke and support reflection around cases will largely rely on their ability to select relevant narratives, design tasks that support teacher reflection, and dialogue with them so as to expand their knowledge and critical abilities. Before beginning case analysis, it will be important to introduce the rationale and principles of pedagogy for autonomy, and also of case pedagogy in teacher education (What justifies the use of cases? How can they support teacher development?). A general approach to case analysis might then involve the following steps:

- Selecting narratives of real experiences within pedagogy for autonomy, based on their innovative nature, enquiry-orientedness, and potential connections with relevant aspects of pedagogy for autonomy (concepts, assumptions, principles, practices, dilemmas...); the number of narratives used in a programme will depend on curriculum contents and goals, time available, the narratives themselves (extension and richness), and the amount of work done with each narrative;
- Proposing individual and collaborative tasks that allow teachers to (re)interpret each narrative with reference to their own teaching or learning experiences (how does it resonate with them?), and also with reference to theoretical input (e.g., an article, a scheme, a definition, etc.) or reflective tools (e.g. Table 6 in section 3.3.2 above on *centring teaching on learning*); narratives should be analysed from different perspectives, so that the question "what is this a case of?" can be explored from various angles, thus enhancing teachers' awareness of the richness and complexity of educational experience, and of possible connections between theory and practice;
- Discussing the outcomes of the tasks with teachers, with the purpose of confronting ideas, negotiating understandings, expanding theoretical input as needed, and reflecting on the feasibility of the case approach in the teachers' own professional contexts; dialogue with teachers should be open and inclusive (everyone's voice counts), and even though negotiation towards shared understandings is important, dissent can also be important as teachers may hold and maintain different views, the main point being that they reflect critically on them;
- Asking teachers to write a journal or portfolio where their reflections on cases are registered, along with ideas for pedagogical experimentation; writing allows teachers to further reflect on cases and the teacher educator can then provide individual feedback on their reflections;
- Involving teachers in the evaluation of case analysis for professional development; this can be done in teachers' journals and portfolios or by using anonymous feedback questionnaires, allowing the teacher educator to collect data so as to dialogue with teachers, and reflect on and improve the approach.

This approach allows teachers to become familiar with unfamiliar teaching approaches, compare and scrutinise experiences, confront personal and public theories, question personal practices, and open up their minds to new practices. The teacher educator is responsible for designing and monitoring the approach, but its development is dialogical and, to a large extent, contingent on teachers' contributions.

One of the problems associated with case analysis is that it is rather time-consuming and may have to be combined with other strategies. Its major shortcoming is that it does not involve pedagogical experimentation and narrative writing, which are the central elements of the strategy that follows.

5.2.2 Developing and writing personal cases

This strategy is about case construction by teachers and has two main components: *enquiry-based pedagogical experimentation* and *narrative writing*. It can be combined with the previous strategy, although it is more suitable for in-service teacher education as it requires teachers to develop and narrate an autonomy-oriented experience. In pre-service teacher education, it can only be implemented in the student teachers' practicum or school placement.

The engagement of teachers in pedagogical enquiry, namely through action research, is one of the crucial elements of reflective teacher development, involving the identification of a problem, dilemma or interest that motivates the development and evaluation of an intervention plan. Supporting teachers to develop autonomy-oriented experiences is a way to enhance experiential professional learning. However, professional learning will be strongly reinforced if teachers further narrate their experience, because writing on the basis of experience can become a method of (self-)discovery through which teachers reinterpret experience and learn more about it and about themselves as educators:

> Writing involves a textual reflection in the sense of separating and confronting ourselves with what we know, distancing ourselves from the lifeworld, decontextualizing our thoughtful preoccupations from immediate action, abstracting and objectifying our lived understandings from our concrete involvements, and all this for the sake of now reuniting us with what we know, drawing us more closely to living relations and situations of the lifeworld, turning thought to more tactful

praxis, and concretizing and subjectifying our deepened understanding in practical action. (Van Manen, 1990: 129)

Professional narratives should illustrate writing *from* the self rather than *about* the self (Contreras & Pérez de Lara, 2010), which means that teachers avoid a confessional, self-legitimating tone by assuming a stance that is both close to lived experience and critically detached from it, thus giving potential readers the opportunity to learn from it.

As in the previous strategy, it will be important to introduce teachers to the rationale and principles of pedagogy for autonomy and case pedagogy. It will also be important to introduce them to the rationale and principles of enquiry-based teaching. A general approach to case construction might involve the following steps:

- Promoting teachers' reflection on their language teaching experiences with reference to theoretical input and practical examples of pedagogy for autonomy (this is where case analysis might be particularly useful);
- Supporting teachers in designing small-scale, autonomy-oriented intervention plans by considering questions such as: What problem, dilemma, interest... motivates me to change my practice and why? What vision of education would I like to enact? What pedagogical questions would I like to answer? What do I need to read? In what context would I like to intervene and why? What strategies and materials will I design? How will I evaluate my plan, i.e. what data collection strategies will I use? What do I expect regarding student learning and my own professional development? What problems can I anticipate and how can I possibly solve them?...
- Supporting teachers in designing teaching and data collection materials to be used in the experiences; this support is extremely important because teachers are innovating their teaching and may have no experience of classroom enquiry; data collection strategies may involve lesson observation and teacher reflective records, student questionnaires and interviews, self-regulation checklists, learning journals and portfolios, and the analysis of student performance in language tasks; it is important to stress that whatever strategies are used, they should combine pedagogical and research purposes (e.g., if a questionnaire on reading strategies is administered to the students, results should be later discussed in class to involve them in further reflection on reading);

- Discussing the experiences with teachers as they implement them with their students; teachers can either develop individual experiences or work in groups, although group work can enhance a collaborative culture of teaching and reinforce the development of teachers' critical skills; group members can all carry out the experience or choose one of the teachers to do it; if experiences are designed in groups and conducted by one teacher in each group, all group members should participate in the analysis of the experience and, if possible, observe its implementation in class; whatever the strategy used, the teacher educator must be able to support and provide feedback to all experiences;
- Supporting teachers in producing narratives of experience, which will be written individually or in groups depending on how experiences are conducted; each narrative must describe and interpret the experience, integrate theoretical input, and answer the question "what is this a case of?"; narratives should be written in a personal style that combines the rigorous analysis of experience with the integration of theoretical knowledge and the use of creative language (analogies, metaphors…); their extension and depth can vary, but they should always illustrate pedagogical enquiry processes and instigate further reflection;
- Involving the teachers in the self-evaluation of their work, on the basis of criteria previously proposed or negotiated (e.g. adequacy of experience to context; enactment of pedagogy for autonomy principles; relevance of data collection strategies; ability to interpret experience on the basis of data collected and theoretical input, etc.);
- Providing written feedback on each narrative, focusing on the same criteria and suggesting improvements; teachers may be asked to revise their narratives according to the teacher educator's feedback, and permission may be asked to use the revised versions with other teachers for case analysis;
- Involving teachers in the evaluation of case construction for professional development; this can be done in teachers' narratives or by using anonymous feedback questionnaires, allowing the teacher educator to collect data so as to dialogue with teachers, and reflect on and improve the approach.

Because case construction is quite demanding on teachers – requiring the articulation between teaching and research, theory and practice, practice and writing – teacher educators' support is of paramount importance. Case construction clearly benefits teacher empowerment because it emerges directly from teachers' concerns and aspirations, requires them to undertake a critical analysis of teaching, engages them in explorations of autonomy, and promotes reflective experiential writing. Their narratives can be used by other teachers (e.g. through case analysis as described above) and disseminated in professional conferences and publications.

5.2.3 Writing teacher education cases from teachers' experience

This strategy was first developed within the European project EuroPAL mentioned in the Introduction. A number of cases were produced by the research team and published in a multilingual DVD (Jiménez Raya & Vieira, 2011). The main difference as compared to the previous strategies is that here cases are written by teacher educators. Moreover, as Jiménez Raya & Vieira (2015: 108) point out, these cases do not present themselves as conventional narratives, but rather as multi-modal texts which combine various types of resources creatively so as to guide a theme-oriented journey of enquiry on the part of the teachers-users, either on their own or in formal teacher education contexts.

Jiménez Raya & Vieira (2015: 106) explain that case writing starts from real teachers' explorations of pedagogy for autonomy (*case teachers*), which teacher educators (*case writers*) interpret together with them, so as to design reflective tasks that help other teachers (*case users*) go through cases with a double focus: the case teachers' experience and their own experience. Theoretical input and practical instruments are added in order to help other teachers interpret each case and expand their pedagogical understanding and expertise as regards pedagogy for autonomy. Suggestions for pedagogical experimentation are offered to encourage them to innovate their teaching along the lines of each case. Based on Jiménez Raya & Vieira (2011, 2015), Figure 3 proposes an overall structure for case writing. Drawing on a narrative metaphor, cases are structured around Themes, Episodes and Scenes:

- The *Theme* is the main focus of the case teacher's experience. Focusing cases on a theme increases case coherence and allows for a smooth combination of theoretical and practical knowledge in a meaningful way.
- Each theme is organised into three *Episodes*: *Understanding the Background*, *Looking at Practice*, and *Exploring Possibilities*. The first epi-

sode introduces the theme and focuses on the case teacher and his/her professional context; the second episode fosters the conceptual development of the theme, along with tasks centred on the case teacher's specific practices for promoting autonomy; the final episode focuses on the case reader by providing suggestions for pedagogical enquiry within the theme and includes his/her self-evaluation of professional development. Episodes are divided into *Scenes* that signal relevant dimensions of each case and help teachers move gradually from a focus on the case teacher's practice to a focus on their own practice, from understanding the illustrated approach to exploring it themselves.

- Episodes and Scenes integrate: (a) *case materials* directly extracted from the case teacher's experience (e.g. teacher/learner reflections, teaching/learning tasks, lesson videoclips, teacher/learner interviews etc.), (b) explanatory/informative *text* related to the case teacher's experience, the proposed tasks and the conceptual/research background, and (c) reflection/action-oriented *tasks* with a focus on various aspects of the case and the teachers' personal professional experience.

Figure 3. Case structure (Jiménez Raya & Vieira, 2011, 2015)

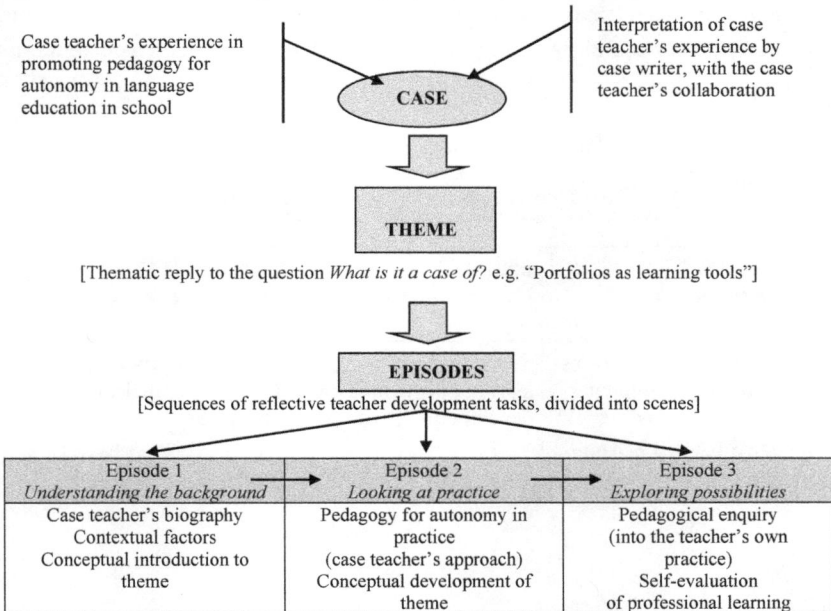

Episode 1 *Understanding the background*	Episode 2 *Looking at practice*	Episode 3 *Exploring possibilities*
Case teacher's biography Contextual factors Conceptual introduction to theme	Pedagogy for autonomy in practice (case teacher's approach) Conceptual development of theme	Pedagogical enquiry (into the teacher's own practice) Self-evaluation of professional learning

Teacher Development Resources [Episodes integrate *case materials*, *text* and *tasks*]		
Case materials ←→	*Text* ←→	*Tasks*
Teacher/learner narratives/reflections Teacher/learner interviews Lesson videoclips/transcripts Teaching/learning materials Classroom/learner data	Foci and goals of episodes Task instructions Theoretical support to tasks Research data	Reflection-oriented Action-oriented (tasks focus on both the case teacher' and the teacher's experience)

From the point of view of the users, this strategy combines case analysis with case construction, because teachers are involved in tasks that aim at analysing the case teacher's experience along with tasks that instigate reflection on and innovation in their own experiences. In order to illustrate the kinds of tasks that can be designed, we present some excerpts from the case summarised in Table 9 (Jiménez Raya & Vieira, 2011), focused on *Portfolios as Learning Tools* and designed around the experience of Antonieta Mamede, a portuguese English teacher who explored portfolios with upper-secondary students (ages 16–17). Although this case was designed for in-service teacher education, teacher educators can also develop cases for pre-service teachers by appealing to their past and current experiences as language learners and their future experience as language teachers.

Table 9. Case on 'Portfolios as Learning Tools' (Jiménez Raya & Vieira, 2011)

CASE THEME: PORTFOLIOS AS LEARNING TOOLS		
Episode 1 *Understanding the background*	Episode 2 *Looking at practice*	Episode 3 *Exploring possibilities*
Scene 1: Teaching priorities and learner development *Scene 2:* What is a learning portfolio?	*Scene 3:* How can learning portfolios be developed?	*Scene 4:* How can I introduce the learning portfolio? *Scene 5:* What have I learnt?

PEDAGOGICAL PRINCIPLES	
• Responsibility, choice, and flexible control • Learning to learn and self-regulation • Integration and explicitness	• Learner differentiation • Reflective enquiry • Formative assessment

Below are examples of tasks designed for this case (Jiménez Raya & Vieira, 2011: 12–20, introductory booklet to cases).

TEACHING PRIORITIES AND LEARNER DEVELOPMENT (EPISODE 1. SCENE 1)

How would you describe a language teacher's job? Try to prioritise the following teaching tasks according to the importance they have for you as a language teacher.
[1 – most important; 8 – least important].

	Develop the students' critical thinking
	Help the students become more self-directed language learners
	Cover the prescribed syllabus and/or textbook
	Prepare the students for tests and exams
	Reflect on practice and find solutions to pedagogical problems
	Foster the students' personal and social growth
	Develop the students' communicative skills in the FL
	Create an atmosphere that motivates students to learn the language

If you can, share your ideas with peers. How do their priorities differ from yours? How do different teaching priorities relate to views of what *learning* a language entails?

Read Antonieta's reflection on her priorities as a language teacher and her views of what language teaching and learning entail [teacher narrative].

(.........)

In her text, Antonieta points out some priorities that make teaching tough and challenging. What problems, constraints or dilemmas may teachers face as they try to enact those priorities?
If you can, discuss this with peers, students, mentors…and add up their ideas.

ANTONIETA'S PRIORITIES	POTENTIAL PROBLEMS, CONSTRAINTS, DILEMMAS
Creating a climate which facilitates the development of learners' full potential and guides them towards autonomy (mutual respect, trust and support; balance in power relationships...)	
Leaving no student behind, by helping everyone become aware of their true potential and objectives, learn how to learn, develop thinking skills and self-direction	
Being a reflective practitioner by experimenting with new approaches, evaluating their impact, making informed choices, and being subversive if necessary	

If you want to reflect further on factors that can affect teaching priorities, especially as regards the development of pedagogy for autonomy, read *Understanding the setting* [information text with reflective questions].

(.........)

Antonieta's approach to putting her priorities into action consists of helping her students develop learning portfolios as a way of promoting their autonomy. What is your idea of a "learning portfolio"? Write your definition here:

About the background to Antonieta's choice to use portfolios, read *Contextualizing my Pedagogical Choices* [teacher narrative].

(.........)

WHAT IS A LEARNING PORTFOLIO? (EPISODE 1. SCENE 2)

According to Costa & Kallick (2004: 65), "a portfolio is a collection of work, developed over time, with an accompanying reflection to show why that work was chosen for the portfolio". This is a very simple definition. However, portfolios entail significant changes in traditional ways of learning and teaching. The activities that follow focus on assumptions and implications of using portfolios.

In your opinion, what is the difference between a *portfolio* and a traditional *file or dossier*? Jot down your ideas below.

Learning portfolio: main features	Traditional File/Dossier: main features

Would you like to read a proposal for the distinction between portfolios and files/dossiers? If so, look at *Portfolios vs. Dossiers* [information text with reflective questions].

(.........)

Imagine that you wanted to propose a *structure* for a language learning portfolio to be developed by your students. Think of the sections they might include in it.

If possible, discuss it with students, peers or mentors.

Portfolio organisation: a proposal

Portfolio sections	Brief explanation of what each section might include

You can look at *Antonieta's proposal*:

Introductory Text	The student introduces her/himself, defines 'portfolio' and explains what s/he expects to achieve with it
Language Passport	The student records qualifications, certificates or diplomas obtained in English, as well as significant language and intercultural experiences

Language Biography	The student assesses her/his language ability using reference levels proposed in the CEF (Council of Europe, 2001a) and makes a personal statement of learning problems and goals for the school-term ahead. Self-assessment grids used during the year are also included here
Dossier	The student presents evidence of progress and efforts to learn more autonomously: self-initiated work and reflections on that work, reasons to do it, satisfaction with results, problems and plans to overcome them (Compulsory work assigned by the teacher is *not* included, as students are expected to identify individual problems and try to solve them as autonomously as possible on the basis of self-reflection). The dossier includes two kinds of items: – Language exercises which students select, do, self-correct, and reflect about (including planning for further work) – Written tasks (letters, essays, reports, etc.) which students choose to do, hand out to me (or any other qualified person) for feedback, self-correct, and reflect about (including planning for further work)

Antonieta's proposal integrates some ideas from the Council of Europe's European Language Portfolio (ELP). Do you know what it is? You can find some information in *The European Language Portfolio* [information text]. You can also go to: http://www.coe.int/en/web/portfolio

(.........)

Self-assessment is a major aspect of Antonieta's approach to learning port-folios, and also a major component of self-regulation:

> Students need the opportunity to look back at their work. Too often, we hear students say, "I already finished that work. What more do you want?" When teachers focus on self-assessment, the question is reversed. It is, "What more do *I* want?" Striving for excellence is a life task, not a singular event to satisfy a teacher. We want to see students develop a love of learning and not depend solely on the judgement of others to determine the value of what they are learning. (Costa & Kallick, 2004: 68)

Self-assessment can be a complement to tests and teacher assessment, and its main potential "is in its use as a tool for motivation and awareness raising: helping learners to appreciate their strengths, recognise their weaknesses and orient their learning more effectively" (Council of Europe, 2001a: 192).

Below are some strategies that can promote the ability to self-assess. Tick those you *(almost) never* promote and think of possible reasons why Antonieta would do it.

√	SELF-ASSESSMENT STRATEGIES	REASONS TO PROMOTE THEM
	Prioritising needs and setting learning goals	
	Identifying desirable learning standards or criteria with reference to learning goals	
	Making learning plans to attain goals (strategies, resources, time, space...)	
	Carrying out learning plans and monitoring learning processes*	
	Revising learning plans as needed	
	Recording and keeping track of progress	
	Self-evaluating performance and outcomes	
	Negotiating final grades with teachers	

* e.g. through rating scales, strategy checklists, reflective records, dialogue with others, etc.)

(.........)

HOW CAN LEARNING PORTFOLIOS BE DEVELOPED? (EPISODE 2. SCENE 3)

At the beginning of each term, Antonieta's students reflect on their strengths and weaknesses as regards language abilities, so that they can decide on what they need to practise more outside class. This kind of self-initiated work goes into the Dossier section in their portfolio, together with a free reflection on why they decided to do it (goals), how it worked (effectiveness and problems) and what they intend to do in the future (plans). Written assignments are usually read by Antonieta for feedback, and students compile different versions of the same item, thus showing evidence of their effort to improve.

Reflection about learning is a key aspect of this approach. However, students often show some resistance towards reflection:

> At the beginning I thought that making so many reflections would be extremely boring, but later I realised that it is very useful in order to identify and correct

125

our mistakes, allowing us to overcome many of our difficulties. (Ana Luísa, final reflection, translated)

Since this type of work is not usual in secondary schools, the preparation of this portfolio brought about some problems at the beginning, as I didn't have the habit of analysing my performance regularly and deeply. However, as time went by, that constraint vanished, and in the end I could do my self-assessment easily and without any fear, which contributed, undoubtedly, to substantial improvement. (João, final reflection, translated)

Teachers may need to support students' reflections, especially at the beginning, and this is what happens with Antonieta:

I often monitor students' reflections so as to help them improve self-assessment skills and check if the activities they decide to do are appropriate to their needs. We also conduct regular conferences to clarify any doubts, help them organise their materials and be more specific in their reflections. (Antonieta's reflection)

The examples below (Costa & Kallick, 2004: 65) provide simple rubrics to support learner reflection. Try using one or more to help your students reflect on a specific task that they have finished recently. They can do it orally or in writing.

The process I went through to create this piece
Who or what influenced me to create this piece
Risks I took in the creation of this piece
New insights I gained about myself as I created this piece
This piece was an experiment for me because...
I have discovered that I am good at...
What continues to intrigue me is...
The evidence that I have that shows my growth is...

How did your students react to the activity? Did *you* learn anything from it?

Have a look at examples of *Joana's reflections in her portfolio* [student reflections with reflective questions].

(.........)

HOW CAN I INTRODUCE THE LEARNING PORTFOLIO? (EPISODE 3. SCENE 4)

The tasks that follow can help you *design, implement and evaluate the introduction of learning portfolios in one of your foreign language classes.* The suggested steps for you to follow are:

- Selecting one class
- Introducing the idea of the portfolio to the class
- Deciding on an overall plan for the portfolio
- Supporting students in starting to make learning plans
- Designing materials to support self-regulation

(.........)

Negotiate an overall initial plan for portfolio development: learning goals, sections and items to include. You can use a grid like the following one:

LEARNING GOALS	SECTIONS	WHAT TO INCLUDE IN EACH SECTION

(.........)

As you negotiate an overall plan to develop portfolios, it might be important to help the students reflect about "who will do what" as regards the learning goals that are agreed upon. The responsibility chart presented below may be used:

LEARNING GOALS	STUDENT'S JOB/ RESPONSIBILITY	SHARED JOB/ RESPONSIBILITY	TEACHER'S JOB/ RESPONSIBILITY

(adapted from Costa & Kallick, 2004: 126)

The same chart may also be used during the process as students become more aware of what building their portfolio entails, and also to monitor performance: "is everyone fulfilling their role as expected?"

(.........)

Time to evaluate your experience! If you kept any notes during its development, go through them. What have you learnt from exploring your practice? What about your students? Where do you both go from here?

I HAVE LEARNT TO...	IT WAS DIFFICULT FOR ME TO...
MY STUDENTS HAVE LEARNT TO...	IT WAS DIFFICULT FOR THEM TO...
OUR NEXT STEPS...	

(.........)

Just as with the previous strategies, using this kind of case in teacher education involves dialogue between teachers and teacher educators around tasks, the provision of further theoretical input as needed, and the involvement of teachers in assessing their value for professional growth. However, these cases are built so as to create conditions for self-directed learning, therefore teachers can go through them on their own as complementary tasks in teacher education programmes or outside those programmes.

These cases represent valuable teacher development resources that combine theory and practice to foster reflective enquiry. Building them is time consuming and requires creativity from teacher educators, as well as experience in designing teacher education tasks. It further requires that teacher educators are willing to learn from and with teachers who are exploring pedagogy for autonomy, and that these teachers are willing to collaborate in case writing. Jiménez Raya & Vieira (2015) suggest that a particularly challenging approach would be to integrate the writing of these cases into teacher education programmes as a core task to be developed by the teachers and the teacher educator. This could also be done within learning communities where teacher educators and teachers work together.

The three strategies presented here as possible realisations of a case-based pedagogy in teacher education are all experience-based and involve various forms of pedagogical and narrative enquiry. We would like to stress their potential for developing a scholarship of teaching in teacher education settings, with a view to enhancing both teacher and learner autonomy.

6. Final remarks

Designing a framework for the development of pedagogy for autonomy in language education in schools raises fundamental questions for which there are no single answers:

- *What are the educational and social goals of schooling, and what are the means that best serve those goals?*
- *What are the educational and social goals of language learning and teaching, and what are the means that best serve those goals?*
- *What is the nature of learning and teaching and how does each develop?*
- *How do, can and should teachers enhance their learners' (and their own) learning?*
- *What is the role of teacher education in promoting teacher and learner empowerment?*

We believe that this book represents a possible starting point for discussing these issues, by arguing in favour of pedagogy for autonomy as a re[ide]alistic practice aimed at enhancing (inter)personal empowerment and social transformation, with implications for how teacher education should be developed.

In presenting our vision of education and proposing a conceptual framework that is intended to promote pedagogical reflection and action, we assume that schools and teacher education institutions are dynamic and evolving organisms and that teachers and teacher educators can be agents of change. However, schools and teacher education institutions are also conservative and hybrid spaces where conflicting interests and rationalities exist (not only pedagogical, but also political and economic), giving rise to tensions and dilemmas that are integral to educational experience. Therefore, there will always be a distance between actual and ideal accomplishments, and it is in the interspace between reality and ideals that re[ide]alistic change may occur.

Because education is a complex, multifaceted field, what pedagogy *is* and *can* be is not only in the hands of teachers and teacher educators. Policymakers, syllabus and materials designers, school managers and educational researchers are also accountable for the quality of school education and responsible for improving the conditions for teaching and learning. This means that other questions need to be added to the ones above, namely:

- *What role do, can and should these educational agents play in the transformation of school pedagogy?*
- *How do, can and should they develop a dialogue with and work with teachers?*
- *How do, can and should their discourses and practices serve the interests of teachers, students, and society at large?*

Again, there are no single answers to these questions. Nevertheless, because we are educational researchers, at this point we would like to suggest the need for educational research to become more socially relevant and transformative by moving away from established canons and agendas that tend to distance researchers from teaching and teachers. Actually, academic research has too often been developed at the margin of teachers and even at their cost, imposing itself as the only legitimate source of valid knowledge (Gore & Gitlin, 2004). Whatever status this kind of research has in academic settings, it is highly questionable whether it has contributed to the transformation of educational policies and practices. Schostak & Schostak (2008: 1) confront us with an unsettling question in this regard: "Is it still possible, or even advisable, to ask why it is that so much research contributes so little to democratic questioning of the powerful? Has research become just a tool for the powerful, the complacent, the satisfied?". What they recommend is a move away from "normal research", which "begins with schooling in instructions to solve puzzles", towards what they call "radical research" which "begins with a drawing out, that is, an education, a calling forth of questions that dis-solve the puzzles", and whose motivation is "to drive democracy further down to individuals engaging with each other, drawing upon their *power* to create community as a facilitator of each other's talents and thus to enrich each other as individuals" (Schostak & Schostak, 2008: 13). This entails looking at what goes wrong in education from a democratic standpoint and involving research participants, including teachers, in an empowering search for education that is more rational and just. As the authors put it (2008: 250), "Addressing 'wrongs' is the radical heart of emancipatory research methodologies and educational practice. (…) It is a return to the beginning: what sort of community is desired?".

The question *What sort of community is desired?* lies at the heart of this book. As we stated in the Introduction, our focus on pedagogy for autonomy in language education is motivated by high aspirations, namely the enhancement of democratic teaching and learning practices within a vision of school (language) education as a space for enacting (inter)personal empowerment and promoting social transformation. Our main intention has been to encourage critical reflection and innovation towards the construction of autonomy-oriented communities, by providing a standpoint from which readers can analyse and expand their own experience. That standpoint entails a democratic stance that results from our own convictions about what education *is*, *can* and *should be*, and even though it is not our purpose to tell teachers or teacher educators what they should think and do, our proposals are, to a large extent, normative-oriented. This is not because we think we know best, but because our commitment to pedagogy for autonomy, which is largely influenced by our own professional histories, necessarily determines the way we initiate dialogue with others *about* and *for* language education, through a discourse that needs to be read critically, discussed, and probed in professional contexts. Only readers can judge and build on our work, which we hope to be inspiring, thought provoking, and relevant.

7. References

Alexander, P. A., & Dochy, F. (1995). Conceptions of knowledge and beliefs: A comparison across varying cultural and educational communities. *American Educational Research Journal, 32,* 413–442.

Ames, C. (1986). Effective motivation: the contribution of the learning environment. In R. S. Feldman (Ed.), *The Social Psychology of Education.* Cambridge: Cambridge University Press.

Anderson, J. R. (1985). *Cognitive Psychology and its Implications* (2nd ed.). New York: Freeman and Company.

Aviram, R. (2000). Beyond constructivism: Autonomy-oriented education. *Studies in Philosophy and Education, 19,* 465–489.

Aviram, R., & Yonah, Y. (2004). 'Flexible control': Towards a conception of personal autonomy for postmodern education. *Educational Philosophy and Theory, 36,* (1), 3–17.

Bailin, S., Case, R., Combs, J. R., & Daniels, L. B. (1999). Conceptualizing critical thinking. *Journal of Curriculum Studies, 31,* (3), 285–302.

Bandura, A. (1986). *Social Foundations of Thought and Action: A Social Cognitive Theory.* Englewood Cliffs, NJ: Prentice Hall.

Bandura, A. (1993). Perceived self-efficacy in cognitive development and functioning. *Educational Psychologist, 28,* 117–148.

Bandura, A. (1997). *Self-Efficacy: The Exercise of Control.* New York: Freeman.

Bandura, A. (2001). Social cognitive theory: An agentic perspective. *Annual Review of Psychology, 52,* 1–26.

Barcroft, J., & Wong, W. (2013). Input, input processing and focus on form. In J. Herschensohn & M. Young-Scholten (Eds.), *The Cambridge Handbook of Second Language Acquisition.* Cambridge: Cambridge University Press.

Barfield, A., & Alvarado, N. D. (Eds.) (2013). *Autonomy in Language Learning: Stories of Practices.* Canterbury: IATEFL Learner Autonomy SIG.

Barfield. A., & Brown, S. (Eds.) (2007). *Reconstructing Autonomy in Language Education – Inquiry and Innovation.* Houndmills: Palgrave Macmillan.

Barfield, A., & Nix, M. (Eds.) (2003). *Autonomy You Ask*. Tokio: The Learner Development Special Interest Group of JALT (The Japan Association for Language Teaching).

Barnett, R., & Coate, K. (2005). *Engaging the Curriculum in Higher Education*. Glasgow: Society for Research into Higher Education and Open University Press.

Baron, J. (1985a). *Rationality and Intelligence*. Cambridge: Cambridge University Press.

Baron, J. (1985b). What kinds of intelligence components are fundamental? In S. F. Chipman, J. W. Segal & R. Glaser (Eds.), *Thinking and Learning Skills*, Vol 2. Hillsdale, NJ: Lawrence Erlbaum Associates.

Bartlett, F. C. (1932). *Remembering*. Cambridge: Cambridge University Press.

Beacco, J. C., Byram, M., Cavalli, M., Coste, D., Cuenat, M. E., Goullier, F., & Panthier, J. (2010). *Guide for the Development and Implementation of Plurilingual and Intercultural Education*. Strasbourg: Council of Europe. Available at: www.coe.int/lang

Benn, S. I. (1976). Freedom, autonomy and the concept of a person, *Proceedings of the Aristotelian Society, LXXVI*, 109–130.

Benson, P. (1997). The philosophy and politics of learner autonomy. In P. Benson & P. Voller (Eds.), *Autonomy and Independence in Language Learning*. London: Longman.

Benson, P. (2000). Autonomy as a learners' and teachers' right. In B. Sinclair, I. McGrath & T. Lamb (Eds.), *Learner Autonomy, Teacher Autonomy: Future Directions*. London: Longman (in association with The British Council).

Benson, P. (2011). *Teaching and Researching Autonomy in Language Learning* (2nd ed.). London: Longman.

Benson, P. (2016). Learner autonomy. In G. Hall (Ed.), *The Routledge Handbook of English Language Teaching*. London: Routledge.

Benson, P., & Voller, P. (Eds.) (1997). *Autonomy and Independence in Language Learning*. London: Longman.

Bereiter, C., & Scardamalia, M. (1989). Intentional learning as a goal of instruction. In L. B. Resnick (Ed.), *Knowing, Learning, and Instruction: Essays in Honor of Robert Glaser*. Hillsdale, NJ: Lawrence Erlbaum Associates.

Bialystok, E. (1994). Analysis and control in the development of second language proficiency. *Studies in Second Language Acquisition, 16,* (2), 157–168.

Black, A. E., & Deci, E. L. (2000). The effects of instructors' autonomy support and students' autonomous motivation on learning organic chemistry: A self-determination theory. *Science Education, 84,* 740–756.

Black, P., & Wiliam, D. (1998). Assessment and classroom learning. *Assessment in Education, 5,* (1), 7–73.

Bobb-Wolff, L., & Vera Batista. J. L. (Eds.) (2006). *Proceedings of the Canarian Conference on Developing Autonomy in the FL Classroom.* La Laguna: University of La Laguna.

Boggiano, A. K., & Katz, P. (1991). Maladaptive achievement patterns in students: The role of teachers' controlling strategies. *Journal of Social Issues, 47,* (4), 35–51.

Bohlinger, S., Haake, U., Jfrgensen, C. H., Toiviainen, H., & Wallo, A. (2015). Conclusion – the contested field of working and learning. In S. Bohlinger, H. Haake, C. H. Jfrgensen, H. Toiviainen & A. Wallo (Eds.), *Working and Learning in Times of Uncertainty – Challenges to Adult, Professional and Vocational Education.* Rotterdam: Sense Publishers.

Boud, D. (1988). Moving towards autonomy. In D. Boud (Ed.), *Developing Student Autonomy in Learning* (2nd ed.). New York: Kogan Page.

Braidi, S. M. (2002). Reexamining the role of recasts in native-speaker/nonnative speaker interactions. *Language Learning, 52,* (1), 1–42.

Breen, M. P., & Littlejohn, A. (2000). The significance of negotiation. In M. P. Breen & A. Littlejohn (Eds.), *Classroom Decision-Making: Negotiation and Process Syllabuses in Practice.* Cambridge: Cambridge University Press.

Brookfield, S. (1985). Self-directed learning: A critical review of research. In S. Brookfield (Ed.), *Self-directed Learning: From Theory to Practice.* New Directions for Continuing Education, No. 25. San Francisco: Jossey Bass.

Brown, D. H. (1994). *Teaching by Principles.* Englewood Cliffs, NJ: Prentice Hall.

Brown, A. L., & Campione, J. C. (1986). Psychological theory and the study of learning disabilities. *American Psychologist, 41,* 1059–1068.

Bygate, M. (2015). Sources, developments and directions of task-based language teaching. *The Language Learning Journal, 44*, (4), 381–400.

Byram, M., & Risager, K. (1999). *Language Teachers, Politics and Cultures.* Clevedon, UK: Multilingual Matters.

Byram, M., & Zarate, G. (1994). *Definitions, Objectives and Assesment of Sociocultural Competence.* Strasbourg: Council of Europe.

Callan, E. (1988). *Autonomy and Schooling.* Kingston: McGill-Queen's University Press.

Callan, E. (1994). Autonomy and alienation. *Journal of Philosophy of Education, 28*, (1), 35–53.

Candy, P. C. (1991). *Self-Direction for Lifelong Learning. A Comprehensive Guide to Theory and Practice.* San Francisco: Jossey-Bass.

Carr, W. (1996). *Una Teoría para la Educación. Hacia una Investigación Crítica de la Educación.* Madrid: Morata.

Chaudron, C. (1985). Intake: On models and methods for discovering learners' processing of input. *Studies in Second Language Acquisition, 7*, (1), 1–14.

Cheetham, G., & Chivers, G. (1996). Towards a holistic model of professional competence. *Journal of European Industrial Training, 20*, (5), 20–30.

Clandinin, D. J. (Ed.) (2007). *Handbook of Narrative Inquiry Methodologies.* Thousand Oaks, CA: Sage.

Clark, I. (2011). Formative assessment: Policy, perspectives and practice. *Florida Journal of Educational Administration and Policy, 4*, (2), 158–180.

Contreras, J. (2002). *A Autonomia de Professores.* São Paulo: Cortez Editora.

Contreras, J., & Pérez de Lara, N. (2010). La experiencia y la investigación educativa. In J. Contreras & N. Pérez de Lara (Eds.), *Investigar la Experiencia Educativa.* Madrid: Ediciones Morata.

Convery, A., & Coyle, D. (1999). *Differentiation and Individual Learners: A Guide for Classroom Practice.* London: CILT.

Cooper, P., & McIntyre, D. (1996). *Effective Teaching and Learning: Teachers' and Students' Perspectives.* Buckingham: Oxford University Press.

Corder, S. P. (1981). *Error Analysis and Interlanguage*. Oxford: Oxford University Press.

Costa, A., & Kallick, B. (2004). *Assessment Strategies for Self-directed Learning*. Thousand Oaks: Corwin Press.

Coterall, S., & Crabbe, D. (Eds.) (1999). *Learner Autonomy in Language Learning: Defining the Field and Effecting Change*. Frankfurt Am Main: Peter Lang.

Council of Europe (2001a). *Common European Framework of Reference for Languages: Learning, Teaching, Assessment*. Cambridge: Cambridge University Press.

Council of Europe (2001b). *European Language Portfolio*. Available at: http://culture2.coe.int/

Cuypers, S. (2004). Critical thinking, autonomy and practical reason. *Journal of Philosophy of Education, 38,* (1), 75–90.

Dam, L. (1995). *Learner Autonomy 3: From Theory to Practice*. Dublin: Authentik.

Dearden, R. F. (1972). Autonomy and education. In R. Dearden, P. Hirst & R. Peters (Eds.), *Education and the Development of Reason*. London: Routledge & Kegan Paul.

Deci, E. L., & Flaste, R. (1995). *Why We Do What We Do: Understanding Self-Motivation*. New York, NY: Penguin Books.

Deci, E. L., Koestner, R., & Ryan, R. M. (1999). A meta-analytic review of experiments examining the effects of extrinsic rewards on intrinsic motivation. *Psychological Bulletin, 125,* (6), 627–668.

Deci, E. L., & Ryan, R. M. (1985). *Intrinsic Motivation and Self-Determination in Human Behavior*. New York, NY: Plenum Press.

Deci, E. L., & Ryan, R. M. (1987). The support of autonomy and the control of behavior. *Journal of Personality and Social Psychology, 53,* 1024–1037.

Deci, E. L., & Ryan, R. M. (2000). The "what" and "why" of goal pursuit: Human needs and the self-determination theory of behavior. *Psychology Inquiry, 11,* (4), 227–268.

Deci, E. L., & Porac, J. (1978). Cognitive evaluation theory and the study of human motivation. In M. R. Lepper & D. Greene (Eds.), *The Hidden Costs of Reward: New Perspectives on the Psychology of Human Motivation*. Hillsdale, N.J.: Erlbaum.

DeKeyser, R. (1993). The effect of error correction on L2 grammar knowledge and oral proficiency. *Modern Language Journal, 77,* (4), 501–514.

DeKeyser, R. (1998). Beyond focus on form: Cognitive perspectives on learning and practicing second language grammar. In C. Doughty & J. Williams (Eds.), *Focus on Form in Classroom Second Language Acquisition.* Cambridge: Cambridge University Press.

Dickinson, L. (1987). *Self-Instruction in Language Learning.* Cambridge: Cambridge University Press.

Doecke, B. (2013). Storytelling and professional learning. *English in Australia, 48,* (2), 11–21.

Donato, R., & McCormick, D. (1994). A sociocultural perspective on language learning strategies: The role of mediation. *The Modern Language Journal, 78,* (4), 453–464.

Doughty, C. (1991). Second language acquisition does make a difference: Evidence from an empirical study of SL relativization. *Studies in Second Language Acquisition, 13,* (3), 431–469.

Doughty, C. (2003). Instructed SLA: Constraints, compensation, and enhancement. In C. Doughty & M. H. Long (Eds.), *Handbook of Second Language Acquisition.* New York: Basil Blackwell.

Doughty, C. J., & Long, M. H. (2003). Optimal psycholinguistic environments for distance foreign language learning. *Language Learning & Technology, 7,* (3), 50–80.

Dworkin, G. (1988). *The Theory and Practice of Autonomy.* Cambridge; New York: Cambridge University Press.

East, M. (2015). Taking communication to task – again: What difference does a decade make?. *The Language Learning Journal, 43,* (1), 6–19.

Edge, J. (1999). Learner autonomy with a focus on the teacher. *Revista Canaria de Estudios Ingleses, 38,* 37–46.

Edgerton, R. (2001). *Education White Paper.* Washington, DD: Pew Forum on Undergraduate Learning.

Ellis, G., & Sinclair, B. (1989). *Learning to Learn English – A Course in Learner Training.* Cambridge: Cambridge University Press.

Ellis, N. (2005). At the interface: Dynamic interactions of explicit and implicit knowledge. *Studies in Second Language Acquisition, 27,* (2), 305–352.

Ellis, R. (1989). Are classroom and naturalistic acquisition the same? A study of the classroom acquisition of German word order rules. *Studies in Second Language Acquisition, 11,* (3), 305–328.

Ellis, R. (1990). *Instructed Second Language Acquisition.* Oxford: Blackwell.

Ellis, R. (2003). *Task-based Language Learning and Teaching.* Oxford: Oxford University Press.

Ellis, R. (2004). The definition and measurement of explicit knowledge. *Language Learning, 54,* 227–275.

Ellis, R. (2005). Principles of instructed language learning. *System, 33,* (2), 209–224.

Ellis, R. (2009). Task-based language teaching: Sorting out the misunderstandings. *International Journal of Applied Linguistics, 19,* (3), 221–246.

Ellis, R., & Shintani, N. (2014). *Exploring Language Pedagogy through Second Language Acquisition Research.* London: Routledge.

Eriksson, R. (1993). *Teaching Language Learning – In-service Training for Communicative Teaching and Self-directed Learning in English as a Foreign Language.* Göteborg: Acta Universitatis Gothoburgensis.

Feuerstein, R., Rand, Y. & Hoffman, M. (1979). *The Dynamic Assessment of Retarded Performers.* Glenview, Illinois: Scots Foresman.

Feuerstein, R., Rand, Y., Hoffman, M., & Miller, R. (1980). *Instrumental Enrichment.* Glenview, Illinois: Scots Foresman.

Flavell, J. H. (1979). Metacognition and cognitive monitoring: A new area of cognitive-developmental inquiry. *American Psychologist, 34,* 906–911.

Flavell, J. H. (1987). Speculations about the nature and development of metacognition. In F. E. Weinert & R. H. Kluwe (Eds.), *Metacognition, Motivation and Understanding.* Hillside, New Jersey: Lawrence Erlbaum Associates.

Fredricks, J. A., Blumenfeld, P. C. & Paris, A. H. (2004). School engagement: Potential of the concept, state of the evidence. *Review of Educational Research, 74,* (1), 59–109.

Freire, P. (1974). *Educación para el cambio social.* Buenos Aires: Tierra Nueva.

Freire, P. (1996). *Pedagogia da Autonomia. Saberes Necessários à Prática Educativa.* São Paulo: Paz e Terra.

Garrett, C. (2011). Defining, detecting, and promoting student engagement in college learning environments. *Transformative Dialogues: Teaching & Learning Journal, 5*, (2), 1–12.

Giroux, H. A. (1988). *Schooling and the Struggle for Public Life: Critical Pedagogy in the Modern Age.* Minneapolis: University of Minnesota Press.

Giroux, H. A. (2013). *When schools become dead zones of the imagination: A critical pedagogy manifesto.* Retrieved on October 15 2013 from http://truth-out.org/opinion/item/18133-when-schools-become-dead-zones-of-the-imagination-a-critical-pedagogy-manifesto

Gore, J. M., & Gitlin, A. D. (2004). [RE]Visioning the academic–teacher divide: Power and knowledge in the educational community. *Teachers and Teaching, 10*, (1), 35–58.

Grolnick W. S., Gurland, S. T., Jacob, K. F, & Decourcey, W. (2000). The development of self-determination in middle childhood and adolescence. Motivating the academically unmotivated: a critical issue for the 21st century. *Review of Educational Research, 70*, 151–80.

Guay, F., Ratelle, C. F., & Chanal, J. (2008). Optimal learning in optimal contexts: The role of self-determination in education. *Canadian Psychology, 49*, (3), 233–240.

Guyer, P. (2003). Kant on the theory and practice of autonomy. *Social Philosophy and Policy, 20*, (2), 70–98.

Hall, G. (Ed.) (2016). *The Routledge Handbook of English Language Teaching.* London: Routledge.

Hargreaves, D. H., Hester, S., & Mellor, F. (1975). *Deviance in Classrooms.* London: Routledge & Kegan Paul.

Hedge, T. (2000). *Teaching and Learning in the Language Classroom.* Oxford: Oxford University Press.

Holec, H. (1979). *Autonomie et Apprentissage des Langues Étrangères.* Strasbourg: Hatier.

Holec, H., & Huttunen, I. (Eds.) (1997). *L'Autonomie de l'Apprennant en langues vivantes/ Learner Autonomy in Modern Languages.* Strasbourg: Council of Europe.

Howatt, A. P. R., & Smith, R. (2014). The history of teaching English as a foreign language, from a British and European perspective. *Language & History, 57*, (1), 75–95.

Hughes, A. (2001). The teaching of language to young learners: Linking understanding and principles with practice. In M. Jiménez Raya, P. Faber, W. Gewehr & A. Peck (Eds.), *Effective Foreign Language Teaching at Primary Level*. Frankfurt am Maim: Peter Lang.

Hymes, D. (1972). On communicative competence. In J. B. Pride & J. Holmes (Eds.), *Sociolinguistics*. Harmondsworth, England: Penguin Books.

James, C., & Garrett, P. (Eds.) (1991). *Language Awareness in the Classroom*. London: Longman.

Jiménez Raya, M. (1997). The use of learning autobiographies in language learning. *Barcelona English Language and Literature Studies, 8*, 83–101.

Jiménez Raya, M. (2002). Diario y desarrollo de la metacognición. In M. Carretero González, E. Hidalgo Tenorio, N. McLaren & G. Porte (Eds.), *A Life in Words*. Granada: Universidad de Granada.

Jiménez Raya, M. (2003). Learning to learn for diverse learners. In M. Jiménez Raya & T. Lamb (Eds.), *Differentiation in the Modern Languages Classroom*. Frankfurt am Main: Peter Lang.

Jiménez Raya, M. (2006). Autonomy support through learning journals. In T. Lamb & H. Reinders (Eds.), *Supporting Independent Language Learning: Issues and Interventions*. Frankfurt-am-Main: Peter Lang.

Jiménez Raya, M. (2007). Developing professional autonomy: A balance between license and responsibility. *Independence, Newsletter of the IATEFL Learner Autonomy Special Interest Group, 40,* 32–33.

Jiménez Raya, M. (2011). Language learner autonomy in a Spanish context. In J. Miliander & T. Trebbi (Eds.), *Educational Policies and Language Learner Autonomy in Schools – A New Direction in Language Education?* Dublin: Authentik.

Jiménez Raya, M. (2013). Exploring pedagogy for autonomy in language education at university: possibilities and impossibilities. In M. Pérez Cañado (Ed.), *Competency-Based Language Teaching in the European Higher Education Area*. New York: Springer.

Jiménez Raya, M. (2014). Lehrerautonomie: Auf dem Weg zu Freiheit und Eigenverantwortung. *Jahrbuch Deutsch als Fremdsprache, 40,* 55–70.

Jiménez Raya, M. (2017). Teacher autonomy and agency: The space of possibility in overcoming external obstacles and internal resistances. In M. Jiménez Raya, J. Martos & G. Tassinari (Eds.), *Learner and Teacher*

Autonomy in Higher Education: Perspectives from Modern Language Teaching. Frankfurt-am-Main: Peter Lang.

Jiménez Raya, M., & Lamb, T. (Eds.) (2003). *Differentiation in the Modern Languages Classroom*. Frankfurt-am-Main: Peter Lang.

Jiménez Raya, M., & Lamb, T. (Eds.) (2008a). *Pedagogy for Autonomy in Language Education: Theory, Practice and Teacher Education*. Dublin: Authentik.

Jiménez Raya, M., & Lamb, T. (2008b). Pedagogy for autonomy in language education: Manifestations in the school curriculum. In M. Jiménez Raya & T. Lamb (Eds.), *Pedagogy for Autonomy in Language Education: Theory, Practice and Teacher Education*. Dublin: Authentik.

Jiménez Raya, Lamb, T., & Vieira, F. (2007). *Pedagogy for Autonomy in Language Education in Europe: Towards a Framework for Learner and Teacher Development*. Dublin: Authentik.

Jiménez Raya, M., & Pérez Fernández, J. M. (2002). Learner autonomy and new technologies. *Educational Media International, 39*, (1), 61–68.

Jiménez Raya, M., & Vieira, F. (2008). Teacher development and learner autonomy: Images and issues from five projects. In M. Jiménez Raya & T. Lamb (Eds.), *Pedagogy for Autonomy in Language Education: Theory, Practice and Teacher Education*. Dublin: Authentik.

Jiménez Raya, M., & Vieira, F. (Eds.) (2011). *Understanding and Exploring Pedagogy for Autonomy in Language Education – A Case-based Approach*. Dublin: Authentik. (Booklet and DVD)

Jiménez Raya, M., & Vieira, F. (2015). *Enhancing Autonomy in Language Education: A Case-based Approach to Teacher and Learner Development*. Berlin/ New York: Mouton de Gruyter.

Johnson, K. (1988). Mistake correction. *English Language Teaching Journal, 42*, 89–96.

Johnson, K. (1995). *Understanding Communication in Second Language Classrooms*. Cambridge: Cambridge University Press.

Johnson, K. (1996). *Language Teaching and Skill Learning*. Oxford: Blackwell.

Johnson, K., & Golombek, P. (2002). Inquiry into experience: Teachers' personal and professional growth. In K. Johnson & P. Golombek (Eds.), *Teachers' Narrative Inquiry as Professional Development*. Cambridge: Cambridge University Press.

Jonassen, D. (1991a). Evaluating constructivist learning. *Educational Technology, 36,* (9), 28–33.

Jonassen, D. H. (1991b) Objectivism versus constructivism: Do we need a new philosophical paradigm? *Educational Technology Research and Development, 39,* (3), 5–14.

Kaikkonen, P. (2001). Intercultural learning through foreign language education. In V. Kohonen, R. Jaatinen, P. Kaikkonen & J. Lehtovaara (Eds.), *Experiential Learning in Foreign Language Education.* London: Longman.

Karlsson, L., Kjisik, F., & Nordlung, J. (Eds.) (2001). *All Together Now.* Helsinki: University of Helsinki Language Centre.

Katz, I., & Assor, A. (2006). When choice motivates and when it does not. *Educational Psychology Review, 19,* (4), 429–442.

Kelly, M., Grenfell, M., Allan, R., Kriza, C., & McEvoy, W. (2004). *European Profile for Language Teacher Education – A Frame of Reference.* Southampton University, UK. Final Report to the European Commission Directorate General for Education and Culture.

Kerr, D. (2002). Devoid of community: Examining conceptions of autonomy in education. *Educational Theory, 52,* (1), 13–25.

Kincheloe, J. (2003). *Teachers as Researchers – Qualitative Inquiry as a Path to Empowerment.* London: Routledge Falmer.

Kleinginna, P. Jr., & Kleinginna A. (1981). A categorized list of motivation definitions, with suggestions for a consensual definition. *Motivation and Emotion, 5,* 263–291.

Knowles, M. (1975). *Self-Directed Learning. A Guide for Learners and Teachers.* Englewood Cliffs: Prentice Hall/Cambridge.

Kohonen, V., Jaatinen, R., Kaikkonen, P., & Lehtovaara, J. (2001). *Experiential Learning in Foreign Language Education.* London: Longman.

Kramsch, C. (1993). *Context and Culture in Language Teaching.* Oxford: Oxford University Press.

Krashen, S. (1981). *Second Language Acquisition and Second Language Learning.* Pergamon: Oxford.

Kumaravadivelu, B. (1999). Theorising practice, practising theory: The role of critical classroom observation. In H. Trapeps-Lomax & I. McGrath (Eds.), *Theory in Language Teacher Education.* London: Longman.

Kumaravadivelu, B. (2001). Toward a postmethod pedagogy. *TESOL Quarterly, 35,* (4), 537–560.

Lamb, T. (1998). Now you are on your own! Developing independent language learning strategies. In W. Gewehr (Ed.), *Aspects of Modern Language Teaching in Europe.* London: Routledge.

Lamb, T. (2000a). Finding a voice – learner autonomy and teacher education in an urban context. In B. Sinclair, I. McGrath & T. Lamb (Eds.), *Learner Autonomy, Teacher Autonomy: Future Directions.* Harlow: Addison Wesley Longman (in association with The British Council).

Lamb, T. (2000b). Reconceptualising disaffection – issues of power, voice and learner autonomy. In G. Walraven, C. Parsons, D. Van Veen & C. Day (Eds.), *Combating Social Exclusion through Education.* Louvain, Belgium and Apeldoorn, Netherlands: Garant.

Lamb, T. (2003). Individualising learning: Organising a flexible learning environment. In M. Jiménez Raya & T. Lamb (Eds.), *Differentiation in the Modern Languages Classroom.* Frankfurt am Main: Peter Lang.

Lamb, T. (2004). Motivated to learn? Relationships between motivation and learner autonomy. Plenary presentation at the conference entitled *Autonomy and language learning: Maintaining control,* held at The Hong Kong University of Science and Technology, Hong Kong, and Zhejiang University, Hangzhou, China, 14–18 June 2004.

Lamb, T. (2005a) Rethinking pedagogical models for e-learning. Paper presented at the *AILA World Congress of Applied Linguistics,* held at the University of Madison Wisconsin, USA, 24–29 July 2005.

Lamb, T. (2005b) *Listening to our Learners' Voices: Pupils' Constructions of Language Learning in an Urban School.* Doctoral thesis: University of Nottingham.

Lamb, T. (2006). Supporting independence: Students' perceptions of self-management. In T. Lamb & H. Reinders (Eds.), *Supporting Independent Language Learning: Issues and Interventions.* Frankfurt-am-Main: Peter Lang.

Lamb, T. (2008). Learner autonomy in eight European countries: Opportunities and tensions in education reform and language teaching policy. In M. Jiménez Raya & T. Lamb (Eds.), *Pedagogy for Autonomy in Language Education: Theory, Practice and Teacher Education.* Dublin: Authentik.

Lamb, T. (2009). Controlling learning: Relationships between motivation and learner autonomy. In R. Pemberton, S. Toogood & A. Barfield (Eds.), *Maintaining Control*. Hong Kong: Hong Kong University Press.

Lamb, T. (2010a). Assessment of autonomy or assessment for autonomy? Evaluating learner autonomy for formative purposes. In A. Paran & L. Sercu (Eds.), *Testing the Untestable in Language and Education*. Clevedon: Multilingual Matters.

Lamb, T. (2010b). La formazione dei docenti per lo sviluppo dell'autonomia dell'apprendente e del docente. In P. Diadori (Ed.), *Formazione, qualità e certificazione per la didattica delle lingue moderne in Europa*. Florence, Italy: Le Monnier.

Lamb, T. (2011). Fragile identities: Exploring learner identity, learner autonomy and motivation through young learners' voices. *Canadian Journal of Applied Linguistics, 14*, (2), 68–85.

Lamb, T. (2012). Language associations and collaborative support: Language teacher associations as empowering spaces for professional networks. *Innovation in Language Learning and Teaching, 6*, (3), 287–308.

Lamb, T. (2017). Knowledge about language and learner autonomy. In J. Cenoz & D. Gorter (Eds.), *Language Awareness and Multilingualism*. ISBN 978–3-319-02239-0. In: *Encyclopedia of Language and Education*. Cham, Switzerland: Springer International Publishing Switzerland.

Lamb, T., & Little, S. (2016). Assessment for autonomy, assessment for learning, and learner motivation: Fostering learner identities. In D. Tsagari (Ed.), *Classroom-based Assessment in L2 Contexts*. Cambridge: Cambridge Scholars Publishing.

Lamb, T., & Reinders, H. (Eds.) (2006). *Supporting Independent Language Learning*. Frankfurt-am-Main: Peter Lang.

Lamb, T., & Reinders, H. (Eds.) (2008). *Learner and Teacher Autonomy: Concepts, Realities, and Responses*. Amsterdam: John Benjamins.

Lamb, T., & Simpson, M. (2003). Escaping from the treadmill: Practitioner research and professional autonomy. *Language Learning Journal, 28*, 55–63.

Leitch, R., & Day, C. (2000). Action research and reflective practice: Towards a holistic view. *Educational Action Research*, *8*, (1), 179–193.

Lindley, R. (1986). *Autonomy*. Atlantic Highlands, NJ: Humanities Press International.

Little, D. (1991). *Learner Autonomy 1 – Definitions, Issues and Problems*. Dublin: Authentik.

Little, D. (2000). We're all in it together: Exploring the interdependence of teacher and learner autonomy. In L. Karlsson, F. Kjisik & J. Nordlung (Eds.), *All Together Now*. Helsinki: University of Helsinki Language Centre.

Little, D. (2004). Democracy, discourse and learner autonomy in the foreign language classroom. *Utbildning & demokrati*, *13*, (3), 105–126.

Little, D., Ridley, J., & Ushioda, E. (2002). *Towards Greater Learner Autonomy in the Foreign Language Classroom*. Dublin: Authentik.

Littlewood, W. (1996). "Autonomy": An anatomy and a framework. *System*, *24*, (4), 427–435.

Long, M. H. (1983). Native speaker/non-native speaker conversation and the negotiation of comprehensible input. *Applied Linguistics, 4*, (2), 126–141.

Long, M. H. (1988). Instructed interlanguage development. In L. M. Beebe (Ed.), *Issues in Second Language Acquisition: Multiple Perspectives*. Cambridge, MA: Newbury House/Harper and Row.

Long, M. H., & Ross, S. (1993). Modifications that preserve language and content. In M. Tickoo (Ed.), *Simplification: Theory and Application*. Singapore: SEAMEO Regional Language Centre.

Lunenberg, M. & Korthagen, F. (2009). Experience, theory, and practical wisdom in teaching and teacher education. *Teachers and Teaching*, *15*, (2), 225–240.

MacLaren, P. (1989). *Life in Schools: An Introduction to Critical Pedagogy in the Foundations of Education*. New York: Longman.

Manzano Vázquez, B. (2016). Teacher development for autonomy: An exploratory review of language teacher education for learner and teacher autonomy. *Innovation in Language Learning and Teaching*, published online Sept 2016, DOI: 10.1080/17501229.2016.1235171

Maslow, A. (1954). *Motivation and Personality*. New York: Harper.

Maslow, A. (1970). *Motivation and Personality* (2nd ed.). New York: Harper & Row.

McCafferty, S. G., Jacobs, G. M., & Iddings, A. C. D (Eds.) (2006). *Cooperative Learning and Second Language Teaching*. Cambridge: Cambridge University Press.

McLaughlin, B. (1987). *Theories of Second Language Learning*. London: Edward Arnold.

Mezirow, J. (1997). Transformative learning: Theory to practice. *New Directions for Adult and Continuing Education, 74,* 5–12.

Miller, L. (Ed.) (2007). *Autonomy in the Classroom*. Dublin: Authentik.

Miliander, J. (2011). Language learner autonomy in a Swedish context. In J. Miliander & T. Trebbi (Eds.), *Educational Policies and Language Learner Autonomy in Schools – A New Direction in Language Education?* Dublin: Authentik.

Murray, G., Gao, X., & Lamb, T. (Eds.) (2011). *Identity, Motivation and Autonomy in Language Learning*. Bristol: Multilingual Matters.

Naiman, N., Frohlich, M., Stern, H., & Todesco, A. (1978). *The Good Language Learner*. Research in Education, 7. Toronto: Ontario Institute for Studies in Education.

Newmann, F. M. (1989). Student engagement and High School reform. *Educational Leadership, 46,* 34–36.

Noels, K. A. (2001). New orientations in language learning motivation: Toward a contextual model of intrinsic, extrinsic, and integrative orientations and motivation. In Z. Dörnyei & R. Schmidt (Eds.), *Motivation and Second Language Acquisition*. Honolulu: University of Hawaii Second Language Teaching and Curriculum Center.

Nunan, D. (1988). *The Learner-centred Curriculum*. Cambridge: Cambridge University Press.

Nunan, D. (Ed.) (1992). *Collaborative Language Learning and Teaching*. Cambridge University Press.

Nunan, D. (2004). *Task-Based Language Teaching*. Cambridge: Cambridge University Press.

O'Malley, J. M., & Chamot, A. U. (1990). *Learning Strategies in Second Language Acquisition*. New York: Cambridge University Press.

Ortega, L. (2009). Sequences and processes in language learning. In M. H. Long & C. J. Doughty (Eds.), *Handbook of Language Teaching*. Malden, MA: Wiley-Blackwell.

Oxford, R. (1990). *Language Learning Strategies – What Every Teacher Should Know*. Boston: Heinle & Heinle Publishers.

Palfreyman, D., & Smith, R. (Eds.) (2003). *Learner Autonomy Across Cultures – Language Education Perspectives*. London: Palgrave. Macmillan.

Paradis, M. (2004). *A Neurolinguistic Theory of Bilingualism*. Amsterdam: John Benjamins.

Paradis, M. (2009). *Declarative and Procedural Determinants of Second Languages*. Amsterdam: John Benjamins.

Pascarella, E. T., & Terenzini, P. T. (1991). *How College Affects Students: Findings and Insights from Twenty Years of Research*. San Francisco: Jossey-Bass.

Pearson, P. D., & Raphael, T. E. (1990). Reading comprehension as a dimension of thinking. In B. F. Jones & L. Idol (Eds.), *Dimensions of Thinking and Cognitive Instruction*. Hillsdale, N.J.: Erlbaum Associates.

Pemberton, R., Li, E., Or, W., & Pierson, H. (1996). *Taking Control – Autonomy in Language Learning*. Hong Kong: Hong Kong University Press.

Peters, M. (2001). Education, enterprise culture and the entrepreneurial self: A Foucauldian perspective. *Journal of Educational Enquiry, 2,* (2), 58–71.

Pica, T. (1983). Adult acquisition of English as a second language under different conditions of exposure. *Language Learning, 33,* (4), 465–97.

Pica, T., Halliday, L., Lewis, N., & Morgenthaler, L. (1989). Comprehensible output as an outcome of linguistic demands on the learner. *Studies in Second Language Acquisition, 11,* 63–90.

Pienemann, M. (1984). Psychological constraints on the teachability of languages. *Studies in Second Language Acquisition, 6,* (2), 186–214.

Rea-Dickins, P., & Germaine, K. (1992). *Evaluation*. Oxford: Oxford University Press.

Reinders, H., & Balcikanli, C. (2011). Learning to foster autonomy: The role of teacher education materials. *Studies in Self-Access Learning Journal, 2* (1), 15–25.

Reeve, J. (2009). Why teachers adopt a controlling motivating style toward students and how they can become more autonomy supportive. *Educational Psychologist, 44,* (3), 159–175.

Reeve, J., & Jang, H. (2006). What teachers say and do to support students' autonomy during a learning activity. *Journal of Educational Psychology, 98,* 209–218.

Reeve, J., Jang, H., Carrell, D., Jeon, S., & Barch, J. (2004). Enhancing students' engagement by increasing teachers' autonomy support. *Motivation and Emotion, 28,* 147–169.

Richards, J., & Farrell, T. (2005). *Professional Development for Language Teachers – Strategies for Teacher Learning.* Cambridge: Cambridge University Press.

Rivers, W. (1987). Interaction as the key to teaching language for communication. In W. Rivers (Ed.), *Interactive Language Teaching.* Cambridge, M.A: Cambridge University Press.

Ryan, R. M., & Deci, E. L. (2000). Self-determination theory and the facilitation of intrinsic motivation, social development, and well-being. *American Psychologist, 55,* (1), 68–78.

Ryan, R. M., & Deci, E. L. (2006). Self-regulation and the problem of human autonomy: Does psychology need choice, self-determination, and will? *Journal of Personality, 74,* (6), 1557–1586.

Rubin, J. (1975). What the "good language learner" can teach us. *TESOL Quarterly, 9,* 41–51.

Rubin, J., & Thomson, I. (1994). *How to Be a More Successful Language Learner* (2nd ed.). Massachusetts: Heinle & Heinle Publishers.

Rutherford, W. E. (1987). *Second Language Grammar: Learning and Teaching.* London: Longman.

Schmidt, R. (1994). Deconstructing consciousness in search of useful definitions for applied linguistics. *AILA Review, 11,* 11–26.

Schmidt, R. (1995). *Attention and Awareness in Foreign Language Learning* (Technical Report No. 9). Hawaii: University of Hawaii Second Language Teaching and Curriculum Center.

Schön, D. (1987). *Educating the Reflective Practitioner.* San Francisco: Jossey-Bass Publishers.

Schostak, J. (2000). Developing under developing circumstances: The personal and social development of students and the process of schooling. In H. Altrichter & J. Elliot (Eds.), *Images of Educational Change*. Buckingham: Oxford Unuversity Press.

Schostak, J., & Schostak, J. (2008). *Radical Research – Designing, Developing and Writing Research to Make a Difference*. London: Routledge.

Schunk, D. H., & Zimmerman, B. J. (1998). *Self-Regulated Learning – From Teaching to Self-Reflective Practice*. New York: The Guilford Press.

Schwienhorst, K. (Ed.) (2016). *Learner Autonomy in Second Language Pedagogy and Research: Challenges and Issues*. Faversham: IATEFL.

Sharwood Smith, M. (1993). Input enhancement in instructed SLA: Theoretical bases. *Studies in Second Language Acquisition, 15*, 165–179.

Shor, I. (1992). *Empowering Education: Critical Teaching for Social Change*. Chicago: The University of Chicago Press.

Shuell, T. J. (1988). The role of the student in learning from instruction. *Contemporary Educational Psychology, 13*, 276–295.

Shulman, L. S. (1992). Toward a pedagogy of cases. In J. Shulman (Ed.), *Case Methods in Teacher Education*. New York: Teachers College Press.

Shulman, L. S. (2002). Making differences: A table of learning. *Change, 34,* (6), 36–44.

Shulman, L. S. (2004a). Theory, practice, and the education of professionals. In S. Wilson (Ed.), *Lee S. Shulman: The Wisdom of Practice. Essays on Teaching, Learning, and Learning to Teach*. San Francisco: Jossey Bass.

Shulman, L. S. (2004b). Just in case: Reflections on learning from experience. In S. Wilson (Ed.), *Lee S. Shulman: The Wisdom of Practice. Essays on Teaching, Learning, and Learning to Teach*. San Francisco: Jossey Bass.

Siegel, H. (1988). *Educating Reason. Rationality, Critical Thinking, and Education*. New York: Routledge.

Simons, P. R. (1992). Constructive learning: The role of the learner. In T. M. Duffy, J. Lowyck, D. Jonassen & T. M. Welsh (Eds.), *Designing Environments for Constructive Learning*. Berlin: Springer-Verlag.

Sinclair, B. (1996). Materials design for the promotion of learner autonomy: How explicit is explicit? In R. Pemberton, E. Li, W. Or & H. Pierson

(Eds.), *Taking Control – Autonomy is Language Learning*. Hong Kong: Hong Kong University Press.

Sinclair, B. (2000) Learner autonomy: The next phase? In B. Sinclair, I. McGrath & T.E. Lamb (Eds.), *Learner Autonomy, Teacher Autonomy: Future Directions*. Harlow: Addison Wesley Longman.

Sinclair, B., McGrath, I., & Lamb, T. (Eds.) (2000). *Learner Autonomy, Teacher Autonomy: Future Directions*. London: Longman.

Skehan, P. (1989). *Individual Differences in Second-Language Learning*. London: Edward Arnold.

Skinner, E. A., Furrer, C., Marchand, G., & Kindermann, T. (2008). Engagement and disaffection in the classroom: Part of a larger motivational dynamic? *Journal of Educational Psychology, 100,* (4), 765–781.

Smith, R. (2000). Starting with ourselves: Teacher-learner autonomy in language learning. In B. Sinclair, I. McGrath & T. Lamb (Eds.), *Learner Autonomy, Teacher Autonomy: Future Directions*. London: Longman (in association with The British Council).

Smith, R., & Erdogan, S. (2008). Teacher-learner autonomy: Programme goals and student-teacher constructs. In T. Lamb & H. Reinders (Eds.), *Learner and Teacher Autonomy: Concepts, Realities and Responses.* Amsterdam: John Benjamins.

Smith, W. C. (2016). An introduction to the global testing culture. In W. C. Smith (Ed.), *The Global Testing Culture. Shaping Education Policy, Perceptions, and Practice.* Oxford: Symposium Books.

Smyth, J. (1987). *A Rationale for Teachers' Critical Pedagogy: A Handbook.* Victoria: Deakin University.

Smyth, J. (1989). Developing and sustaining critical reflection in teacher education. *Journal of Teacher Education, 40,* (2), 2–9.

Smyth, J. (1997). Teaching and social policy: Images of teaching for democratic change. In B J. Biddle, T. L. Good & I. F. Goodson (Eds.), *International Handbook of Teachers and Teaching.* Dordrecht: Kluwer Academic Publishers.

Spratt, M., Humphries, G., & Chan, V. (2002). Autonomy and motivation: Which comes first? *Language Teaching Research, 6,* (3), 245–66.

Stefanou, C. R., Perencevich, K. C., DiCintio, M., & Turner, J. C. (2004). Supporting autonomy in the classroom: Ways teachers encourage student decision making and ownership. *Educational Psychologist, 39*, (2), 97–110.

Stern, H. H. (1992). *Issues and Options in Language Teaching*. Oxford: Oxford University Press.

Sternberg, R. J. (1985). Instrumental and componential approaches to the nature and training of intelligence. In S .F. Chipman, J. W. Segal & R. Glaser (Eds.), *Thinking and Learning Skills*, Vol 2. Hillsdale, N.J.: Lawrence Erlbaum Associates, Publishers.

Sternberg, R. J. (1990). *Metaphors of Mind: Conceptions of the Nature of Intelligence*. New York: Cambridge University Press.

Swain, M. (1995). Three functions of output in second language learning. In G. Cook & B. Seidlhofer (Eds.), *Principle and Practice in Applied Linguistics: Studies in Honour of H.G. Widdowson*. Oxford: Oxford University Press.

Sykes G., Bird, T., & Kennedy, M. (2010). Teacher education: Its problems and some prospects. *Journal of Teacher Education, 61*, (5), 464–476.

Tan, K. (2004). Does student self-assessment empower or discipline students? *Assessment and Evaluation in Higher Education, 19*, (6), 651–662.

Tabachnick, R., & Zeichner, K. (Eds.) (1991). *Issues and Practices in Inquiry-oriented Teacher Education*. London: The Falmer Press.

Thavenius, C. (1999). Teacher autonomy for learner autonomy. In S. Cotterall & D. Crabbe (Eds.), *Learner Autonomy in Language Learning: Defining the Field and Effecting Change*. Bayreuth Contributions to Glottodidactics, vol. 8. Frankfurt-am-Main: Peter Lang.

Thomas, H., & Legutke, M. (1991). *Process and Experience in the Language Classroom*. London: Longman.

Tom, A. (1985). Inquiring into inquiry-oriented teacher education. *Journal of Teacher Education, XXXVI*, (5), 35–44.

Trebbi, T. (2011). Language learner autonomy in a Norwegian context. In J. Miliander & T. Trebbi (Eds.), *Educational Policies and Language Learner Autonomy in Schools – A New Direction in Language Education?* Dublin: Authentik.

Towell, R. (2013). Learning mechanisms and automatization. In J. Herschensohn & M. Young-Scholten (Eds.), *The Cambridge Handbook of Second Language Acquisition*. Cambridge; New York: Cambridge University Press.

Tudor, I. (1996). *Learner-Centredness as Language Education.* Cambridge: Cambridge University Press.

Ullmann-Margalit, E., & Morgenbesser, S. (1977). Picking and choosing. *Social Research, 44,* 757–785.

Umbach, P. D., & Wawrzynski, M. R. (2005). Faculty do matter: The role of the college faculty in student learning and engagement. *Research in Higher Education, 46,* (2), 153–184.

UNESCO, *Education 2030. Incheon Declaration and Framework for Action for the Implementation of Sustainable Development Goal 4 – Ensure Inclusive and Equitable Quality Education and Promote Lifelong Learning Opportunities for All.* http://unesdoc.unesco.org/images/0024/002456/245656E.pdf

Ushioda, E. (1996). *Learner Autonomy 5 – The Role of Motivation.* Dublin: Authentik.

Van Lier, L. (1996). *Interaction in the Language Curriculum – Awareness, Autonomy and Authenticity.* London: Longman.

Van Manen, M. (1990). *Researching Lived Experience – Human Science for an Action Sensitive Pedagogy.* London: State University of New York Press.

VanPatten, B., & Williams, J. (2006). *Theories in Second Language Acquisition: An Introduction.* Mahwah, N.J.: Lawrence Erlbaum Associates.

Vansteenkiste, M., Simons, J., Lens, W., Sheldon, K. M., & Deci, E. L. (2004). Motivating learning, performance, and persistence: The synergistic role of intrinsic goals and autonomy-support. *Journal of Personality and Social Psychology, 87,* (2), 246–260.

Vaughan, M., & Burnaford, G. (2016). Action research in graduate teacher education: A review of the literature 2000–2015. *Educational Action Research, 24,* (2), 280–299.

Victori, M. (1999). Methodological issues in research on learners' beliefs about language learning. Paper delivered at the 12th World Congress on Applied Linguistics, Tokyo, Japan, 1–6 August 1999.

Vieira, F. (1997). Pedagogy for autonomy – exploratory answers to questions any teacher should ask. In M. Müller-Verweyen (Ed.), *Standpunkt zur Sprach-und Kulturvermittlung 7: Neues Lernen, Selbstgesteuert, Autonom,* Munique: Goethe Institut.

Vieira, F. (1998). *Autonomia na Aprendizagem da Língua Estrangeira.* Braga: Universidade do Minho.

Vieira, F. (2003). Addressing constraints on autonomy in school contexts – Lessons from working with teachers. In R. Smith & D. Palfreyman (Eds.), *Learner Autonomy Across Cultures – Language Education Perspectives.* London: Palgrave. Macmillan.

Vieira, F. (2006). Understanding and developing pedagogy for autonomy: What are we missing? Proceedings of *The Canarian Conference on Developing Autonomy in the Classroom: Each Piece of the Puzzle Enriches us All.* Canarias: Consejeria de Educación, Cultura y Deportes (CDRom).

Vieira, F. (Ed.) (2009). *Struggling for Autonomy in Language Education – Reflecting, Acting, and Being.* Frankfurt-am-Main: Peter Lang.

Vieira, F. (2010). Pedagogy for autonomy in language education: A re(ide)alistic pratice. Plenary talk presented at the *International TESOL Arabia Conference 2010,* Zayed University (Dubai), March.

Vieira, F. (2011). Language learner autonomy in a Portuguese context. In J. Miliander & T. Trebbi (Eds.), *Educational Policies and Language Learner Autonomy in Schools – A New Direction in Language Education?* Dublin: Authentik.

Vieira, F. (Ed.) (2014a). *Re-conhecendo e Transformando a Pedagogia: Histórias de superVisão.* Santo Tirso: De Facto Editores.

Vieira, F. (Ed.) (2014b). *Quando os Professores Investigam a Pedagogia. Em Busca de uma Educação mais Democrática.* Mangualde: Pedago.

Vieira, F., & Moreira, M. A. (1993). *Para Além dos Testes... A Avaliação Processual na Aula de Inglês.* Braga: Universidade do Minho.

Vieira, F., Moreira, M. A., Barbosa, I., Paiva, M., & Fernandes, I. S. (2010). *No Caleidoscópio da Supervisão – Imagens da Formação e da Pedagogia* (2nd ed.). Mangualde: Edições Pedago.

Vygotsky, L. S. (1962). *Thought and Language.* Cambridge, MA: The M.I.T. Press.

Vygotsky, L. S. (1978). *Mind in Society: The Development of Higher Psychological Processes.* Boston: Harvard Educational Press.

Weiner B. (1992). *Human Motivation: Metaphors, Theories, and Research.* Newbury Park, CA: Sage.

Weinert, F. E., & Kluwe, R. H. (Eds.) (1987). *Metacognition, Motivation, and Understanding*. New Jersey: Lawrence Erlbaum.

Wenden, A. (1991). *Learner Strategies for Learner Autonomy*. New York: Prentice Hall International.

Wenden, A. (1999a). An introduction to metacognitive knowledge and beliefs in language learning: Beyond the basics. *System, 27*, (4), 435–442.

Wenden, A. (1999b). Metacognitive knowledge and language learning. *Applied Linguistics, 19*, (4), 515–537.

Wenden, A. (2002). Learner development in language learning. *Applied Linguistics, 23,* (1), 32–55.

Wenden, A., & Rubin, J. (Eds.) (1987). *Learner Strategies in Language Learning*. New York: Prentice-Hall International.

Williams, G. C., Grow, V. M., Freedman, Z. R., Ryan, R. M., & Deci, E. L. (1996). Motivational predictors of weight loss and weight-loss maintenance. *Journal of Personality and Social Psychology, 70*, (1), 115–126.

Willis, J. (1996). *A Framework for Task-Based Learning*. Harlow: Longman.

Zeichner, K. (1983). Alternative paradigms of teacher education. *Journal of Teacher Education, XXXIV*, (3), 3–9.

Zeichner, K., & Conklin, H. G. (2008). Teacher education programs as sites for teacher preparation. In M. Cochran-Smith, S. Feiman-Nemser, D. J. McIntyre, & K. E. Demers (Eds.), *Handbook of Research on Teacher Education*. New York: Routledge.

Zeichner, K., & Liston, D. P. (1996). *Reflective Teaching: An Introduction*. Mahwah (New Jersey): Lawrence Erlbaum Associates.

Zimmerman, B. J. (1989). A social cognitive view of self-regulated academic learning. *Journal of Educational Psychology, 81*, 329–339.

Zimmerman, B. J. (1998). Developing self-fulfilling cycles of academic regulation: An analysis of exemplary instructional models. In D. H. Schunk & B. J. Zimmerman (Eds.), *Self-Regulated Learning – From Teaching to Self-Reflective Practice*. New York: The Guilford Press.

Zimmerman, B. J. (2002). Becoming a self-regulated learner: An overview. *Theory into Practice, 41*, (2), 64–70.

Zimmerman, B. J., & Risemberg, R. (1997). Self-regulatory dimensions of academic learning and motivation. In G. D. Phye (Ed.), *Handbook of Academic Learning: Construction of Knowledge*. New York: Academic Press.

Foreign Language Teaching in Europe

Edited by:
Manuel Jiménez Raya, Terry Lamb and Flávia Vieira

Vol.   1   Pamela Faber / Wolf Gewehr / Manuel Jiménez Raya / Antony Peck (Eds.): English Teacher Education in Europe. New Trends and Developments. 1999.

Vol.   2   Stephan H. Gabel: Über- und Unterrepräsentation im Lernerenglisch. Untersuchungen zum Sprachgebrauch deutscher Schülerinnen und Schüler in interkulturellen Telekommunikationsprojekten. 2000.

Vol.   3   Winfried Bredenbröker: Förderung der fremdsprachlichen Kompetenz durch bilingualen Unterricht. Empirische Untersuchungen. 2000.

Vol.   4   Manuel Jiménez Raya / Pamela Faber / Wolf Gewehr / Antony J. Peck (eds.): Effective Foreign Language Teaching at the Primary Level. 2001.

Vol.   5   Yvette Coyle / Mercedes Verdú / Marisol Valcárcel: Teaching English to Children - Interactivity and Teaching Strategies in the Primary FL Classroom. 2002.

Vol.   6   Markus Kötter: Tandem learning on the Internet. Learner interactions in virtual online environments (MOOs). 2002.

Vol.   7   Manuel Jiménez Raya / Terry Lamb (eds.): Differentiation in the Modern Languages Classroom. 2003.

Vol.   8   Kees van Esch / Oliver St. John (eds.): A Framework for Freedom. Learner Autonomy in Foreign Language Teacher Education. 2003.

Vol.   9   Kees van Esch / Oliver St. John (eds.): New Insights into Foreign Language Learning and Teaching. 2004.

Vol.   10   Manuel Jiménez Raya / Lies Sercu (eds.): Challenges in Teacher Development: Learner Autonomy and Intercultural Competence. 2007.

Vol.   11   Flávia Vieira (ed.): Struggling for Autonomy in Language Education. Reflecting, Acting, and Being. 2009.

Vol.   12   María Luisa Pérez Cañado / Juan Ráez Padilla (eds.): Digital Competence Development in Higher Education. An International Perspective. 2014.

Vol.   13   Michał B. Paradowski (ed.): Productive Foreign Language Skills for an Intercultural World. A Guide (not only) for Teachers. 2015.

Vol.   14   Manuel Jiménez Raya / José Javier Martos Ramos / Maria Giovanna Tassinari (eds.): Learner and Teacher Autonomy in Higher Education: Perspectives from Modern Language Teaching. 2017.

Vol.   15   Hermann Funk / Manja Gerlach / Dorothea Spaniel-Weise (eds.): Handbook for Foreign Language Learning in Online Tandems and Educational Settings. 2017.

Vol.   16   Manuel Jiménez Raya / Terry Lamb / Flávia Vieira: Mapping Autonomy in Language Education. A Framework for Learner and Teacher Development. 2017.

www.peterlang.com